An Alternate Style: Options in Composition

HAYDEN WRITING SERIES

ROBERT W. BOYNTON, *Consulting Editor*

An Alternate Style: Options in Composition

WINSTON WEATHERS

HAYDEN BOOK COMPANY, INC.

Rochelle Park, New Jersey

Dedicated to Priscilla and Gary Tate

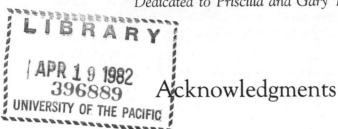

Acknowledgments

A portion of this book was originally published in *Freshman English News*, Winter, 1976, under the title "The Grammars of Style: New Options in Composition."

From *Silence* by John Cage. Copyright © 1958, 1961 by John Cage. Reprinted by permission of Wesleyan University Press.

"Graduation Brain Waves" by Laura Egbert. Reprinted by permission of Laura Egbert.

"The Last Parade," from *Two Cheers for Democracy*, by E. M. Forster. Copyright 1951 by E. M. Forster; renewed 1979 by Donald Parry. Reprinted by permission of Harcourt Brace Jovanovich, Inc., and Edward Arnold (Publishers) Ltd.

"Ezra Pound" by Jamy Fox. Reprinted by permission of Jamy Fox.

Library of Congress Cataloging in Publication Data

Weathers, Winston.
  An alternate style.

  Bibliography: p.
  1. English language—Style. 2. English language—
Rhetoric—Study and teaching. I. Title.
PE1421.W37   808'.042   80-18325
ISBN 0-8104-6130-7

1	2	3	4	5	6	7	8	9	PRINTING
80	81	82	83	84	85	86	87	88	YEAR

Preface

You write. Read. Teach. Speak with other teachers of English about your/their writing, reading, teaching.

You write down your thoughts, observations. Try things in class. Are amazed. Are illuminated.

You publish an article (in *Freshman English News*). Receive response. Encouragement. Gary and Priscilla Tate encourage you. Donald Stewart encourages you.

Other teachers write: "We tried your Grammar B in class. We surprised ourselves. We had great fun. We were liberated."

Students begin to use Grammar B in other classes—in literary criticism, in history, in journalism. (One student even sells a Grammar B essay to a magazine.)

You want to say more. Find more examples. Make additional points. Refine and polish.

And especially show how writers—respected, published authors taught in high schools and colleges—have used the alternate style. Successfully. Seriously. Beautifully. Intelligently.

You expand the article, try to bring home the point that Grammar B is really very practical, very natural. Belongs in the family. Has its place. Must no longer be ignored. The desegregation of style is imperative. Now!

And so this book. Its content tested and retested. Ready to be shared—as we become aware of more mentalities than one (left brain/right brain if nothing else), aware of more compositional goals than one, more life-styles than one, more human chemistries than one, more "voices" than one.

And you are grateful: Robert Boynton has understood, advised, edited, made the book possible.

You offer the book to those who yearn for greater expression. Who love language and want to run with it all the way—all the way round the composition course. Exploring the possibilities. Unafraid. Keeping the word alive. Letting it flourish in all its dimensions.

And you have faith: those who understand will understand . . . and will begin to write, to teach . . . in larger, more open ways.

WINSTON WEATHERS

Tulsa, Oklahoma

Contents

PART FOUR

Introduction

Among the scattered papers of the late Professor X, I have found these jottings.
Did some student write them or did Professor X compose them himself?

Words on paper/one of the ways I—the human being—communicate. There are all the other ways, of course. Talking. Gesturing. Moving my body. Costuming my flesh. Participating in events "out there"/in observable actions. But tremendously important always/words on paper/the string of words in the code of written language, effecting the composition—the "thing made"/the verbal artifact—that I transmit to others for them to negotiate into the miracle of understanding what it is/has been inside the otherwise inaccessible regions of my very human, mysterious brain.

To communicate/but not simply information and data. Not simply knowledge. But emotion, too. Attitude. Stance. Even style and manner themselves. "Look," I often want to say, "This is anger!" "This is confusion!" "This is enigma!" "This is the way I see the universe—mixed up, ambiguous, disorderly." Or "simplistic, barren, vacant." Or "complex, baroque, impenetrable." Even, at times, I want to say, "The message is: there is 'no message.'"

I write for many reasons, to communicate many things. And yet, much of what I wish to communicate does not seem to be expressible within the ordinary conventions of composition as I have learned them and mastered them in the long years of my education. As I grow older, more experienced, perhaps even more mature, I sense that many of the things I want to say do not always "fit" into the communication vehicles I have been taught to construct.

What I've been taught to construct is: the well-made box. I have been taught to put "what I have to say" into a container that is always remarkably the same, that—in spite of varying decorations—keeps to a basically conventional form: a solid bottom, four upright sides, a fine-fitting lid. Indeed, I may be free to put "what I have to say" in the plain box or in the ornate box, in

1

the large box or the small box, in the fragile box or in the sturdy box. But always *the box*—squarish or rectangular. And I begin to wonder if there isn't somewhere a round box or oval box or tubular box, if somewhere there isn't some sort of container (1) that will allow me to package "what I have to say" without trimming my "content" to fit into a particular compositional mode, (2) that will actually encourage me to discover new things to say because of the very opportunity a newly-shaped container gives me (even though I can never escape containers—e.g., syntax—altogether), (3) that will be more suitable perhaps to my own mental processes, and (4) that will provide me with a greater rhetorical flexibility, allowing me to package what I have to say in more ways than one and thus reach more audiences than one.

Occasionally, a wise teacher of composition will acknowledge, "Yes, there are other ways of writing," other voices in other rooms, but the same wise teacher rarely ventures (is it possible? is it permissible?) to explain and demonstrate the "other ways" and provide me with a more extensive range of compositional forms, grammars, vehicles. More frequently, I am told—I who have read Joyce and Stein and Barth and Barthelme and Woolf and Wolfe— that I must distinguish between "creative writing" (nice for Sunday outings into the realms of poetry and fiction) and "ordinary composition" (very practical, young man, for making a living and selling your goods and communicating with all the good decent folks hereabout). That "you should learn to walk before you learn to swim." That if I have talent I may want to take a course in creative writing (it's an elective), but "don't think it's going to save you from the 500-word theme or the second-semester research paper."

But I'm not asking for that. I'm asking simply to be exposed to, and informed about, the full range of compositional possibilities. That I be introduced to all the tools, right now, and not be asked to wait for years and years until I have mastered right-handed affairs before I learn anything about left-handed affairs. That, rather, I be introduced to all the grammars/vehicles/tools/ compositional possibilities *now* so that even as I "learn to write" I will have before me as many resources as possible. I'm asking: that all the "ways" of writing be spread out before me and that my education be devoted to learning how to use them.

PART ONE

1

One of our major tasks as teachers of composition is to identify compositional options and teach students the mastery of the options and the liberating use of them. We must identify options in all areas in vocabulary, usage, sentence forms, dictional levels, paragraph types, ways of organizing material into whole compositions: options in all that we mean by style. Without options, there can be no rhetoric, for there can be no adjustment to the diversity of communication occasions that confront us in our various lives.

To identify options we must not only know about those already established in the language but we must also be alert to emerging ones, and in some cases we must even participate in creating options that do not yet exist but which would be beneficial if they did. We must never suppose that the options in front of us represent the complete and final range of possibilities and that now we can relax: that because we have options enough to avoid rigidity and totalitarianism that we have thus fulfilled our obligations to do all we can to free the human mind and the communication issuing from it.

Most of us do, of course, make options available to our students. Most of us have long shucked off the prescriptions and strictures of an earlier day that gave us no choice in how to write but insisted only on the "one good way." Most of us who teach writing attempt to provide our students with a repertoire of writing styles—from the plain to the elegant, from the tough to the sweet, from the colloquial to the formal, from the simple to the complex—in order that our students may make more refined stylistic decisions in consideration of subject matter, audience, occasion, and so forth. Many of us have argued for many years now that our task is to reveal to our students a full range of styles and to provide them with a rationale for making appropriate selections from that range.

Yet even in our acceptance and inculcation of pluralism and diversity, we stay—if we stop and think about it—within the safe confines of a general "grammar of style," a grammar/a syndrome/a configuration within which our options are related one to another, all basically kin, none of which takes us outside a certain approved and established area.

By "grammar of style" I mean the "set of conventions governing the construction of a whole composition; the criteria by which a writer selects the stylistic materials, method of organization and development, compositional pattern and structure he is to use in preparing any particular composition." This "grammar" defines and establishes the boundaries in which a composition must take place, defines the communication goals to which a composition is committed, and—obviously—the style in which the composition is written.

Any number of such "grammars" or "stylistic families" may theoretically exist and be available to a writer at any one time. Yet on a practical level, in today's classroom we keep all our stylistic options within the confines of one grammar only—a grammar that has no particular name (we can call it the "traditional" grammar of style/or for my purposes Grammar A) but has the characteristics of continuity, order, reasonable progression and sequence, consistency, unity, etc. We are all familiar with these characteristics, for they are promoted in nearly every English textbook and taught by nearly every English teacher.

Our assumption—regardless of liberality so far as diversity of styles is concerned—is that every composition must be well organized and unified, must demonstrate logic, must contain well-developed paragraphs; that its structure will manifest a beginning, middle, and end; that the composition will reveal identifiable types of order; that so far as the composition deals with time it will reveal a general diachronicity; etc. Our teaching and texts will be concerned, almost without exception, with "subject and thesis," "classification and order," "beginning and ending," "expansion," "continuity," "emphasis," and the like. All remains, in other words, within a particular grammar of style that leads to compositions that "make sense": it is a grammar/a syndrome that cannot tolerate a mixed metaphor because a mixed metaphor is not "reasonable," and cannot tolerate a mixture of the impersonal third-person "one" and the impersonal "you" because that would be "inconsistent" and contrary to "unity."

We allow options "within reason." We allow options, but only those that fit within a particular box.

In our charity, we allow our students to write in one style or another—

Arriving in London in the spring of 1960, when crocuses were first blooming in Regency Park, I went directly to the Mount Royal Hotel (the hostelry that many an American tourist knows very well, located as it is on Oxford Street, near the Marble Arch and Hyde Park and conveniently located near everything the American tourist wants to see) where I registered for a room and indicated my intention to stay for seven or eight weeks at least.

I arrived in London in the spring of 1960. Crocuses were blooming in Regency Park. I went directly to the Mount Royal Hotel. It's located on

Oxford Street, near Marble Arch and Hyde Park. It's convenient to a lot of things the American tourist wants to see. I checked in at the hotel and told the clerk I was going to stay in London seven or eight weeks at least.

—but both must do just about the same thing. You can try to write like Henry James or you can try to write like Ernest Hemingway, but you must not forget that both James and Hemingway, quite different in their literary styles, wrote within the same "grammar of style"; neither of them went beyond the parameters that Grammar A provides.

It is as though we told a cardplayer that his deck of fifty-two cards (equal let's say to the "things we can do with language, our stylistic materials") is good only for playing the game of bridge. As good teachers, we explain the rules of bridge and at the same time point out to the student/player his options within bridge: he can play the Culbertson system or the Goren system or the Jacoby system. And indeed he can play his bridge hands even contrary to best advice if he himself so decides, though tradition and good sense usually suggest that he draw trumps early in the hand and play second hand low. We teach him to play bridge, to practice a certain freedom within it (he can conceivably play "high style" or "low style" or "middle style") but there is no way under the sun that he can, in playing bridge, meld a pinochle or "shoot the moon."

Not that anyone really argues that while playing bridge one should not play bridge. But our fault is that we teach students to play bridge only and to have access only to the options that bridge provides. We teach only one "grammar of style" and we provide only square/rectangular boxes. We don't teach students other games with other options. And in our teaching, when someone does "meld a pinochle" at the bridge table, all we know to do is to mark it in red ink and say "wrong," without ever suggesting to the student that if he wants to meld pinochle he might like to know about *another game* where it would be very right.

We identify our favored "grammar of style," our favored game and box, as the "good" grammar of style, and we identify what it produces as "good writing." Martin Joos puts it very well in *The Five Clocks*, his linguistic excursion into the five styles of English usage:

It is still our custom unhesitatingly and unthinkingly to demand that the clocks of language all be set to Central Standard Time. And each normal American is taught thoroughly, if not to keep accurate time, at least to feel ashamed whenever he notices that a clock of his is out of step with the English Department's tower-clock. Naturally he avoids looking aloft when he can. Then his linguistic guilt hides deep in his subconscious mind and there secretly gnaws away at the underpinnings of his public personality. Freud or Kinsey may have strengthened his private self-respect, but in his social life he is still in uneasy bondage to the gospel according to Webster as expounded by Miss Fidditch.

And anything that looms on the horizon as a distinctly different possibility we generally attack as "bad writing" or identify as "creative writing which we don't teach in this class" or ignore altogether, claiming it is a possibility that only rare persons (like James Joyce or Gertrude Stein) could do anything with and that ordinary mortals should scrupulously avoid.

Yet there it is. The beast sniffing outside the door. And ultimately we must deal with it.

It is, of course, *another* grammar/community of style, *another* set of conventions and criteria, *another* way of writing that offers yet more options and offers us yet further possibilities for rhetorical adaptations and adjustments. It is not just another style—way out on the periphery of our concerns—but is an altogether different "grammar" of style, an alternate grammar, Grammar B, with characteristics of variegation, synchronicity, discontinuity, ambiguity, and the like. It is a mature and alternate (*not* experimental) style used by competent writers and offering students of writing a well-tested set of options that, added to the traditional grammar of style, will give them a much more flexible voice, a much greater communication capacity, a much greater opportunity to put into effective language all the things they have to say.

And be assured: Grammar B in no way threatens Grammar A. It uses the same stylistic deck of fifty-two cards and embraces the same English language we are familiar with. Acknowledging its existence and discovering how it works and including it in our writing expertise, we simply become better teachers of writing, making a better contribution to the intellectual and emotional lives of our students.

2

An "alternate style" actually has been present in Anglo-American writing for quite some time now, at least since the end of the eighteenth century, though its presence has generally been obscured by the simple relegation of it to fiction and poetry. Until recent times, it has seldom been tolerated outside "imaginative writing," and even within "imaginative writing" it has been considered simply an eccentricity by a "few crazy writers," not to be taken seriously by anyone else. Laurence Sterne's violation of narrative in *Tristram Shandy* provides great fun, but surely no one would suggest that some of Sterne's tricks and his overall manner might be considered a useful part of every writer's stylistic know-how—would they?

Relegation of Grammar B to fiction and poetry did not mean, however, that Grammar B was never used as an acceptable alternative in prose nonfiction. There are instances where writers did dare to use Grammar B in lieu of A, even in Grammar A's supposedly sacrosanct territories. Such writers in the nineteenth century as William Blake (in the prefatory remarks to each book of *Jerusalem*, for instance) and Walt Whitman (in the 1855 Preface to *Leaves of Grass* and in *An American Primer*) and such writers as D. H. Lawrence (certainly in *Studies in Classic American Literature*) and Gertrude Stein (in such essays as "Reflection on the Atomic Bomb," "Descriptions of Literature," *et al.*) in the twentieth century demonstrated the use of Grammar B in prose nonfiction efforts. (Interestingly enough, Lawrence's statement in "The Spirit of the Place," first chapter in *Studies in Classic American Literature*, is, though dealing with American literary content, very *a propos* to the grammar of style in which he is writing: "It is hard," he says, "to hear a new voice, as hard as it is to listen to an unknown language. . . . Why?—Out of fear. The world fears a new experience more than it fears anything. Because a new experience displaces so many old experiences. And it is like trying to use muscles that have perhaps never been used, or that have been going stiff for ages. It hurts horribly.")

The efforts of such earlier prose practitioners gave the necessary precedent for bringing Grammar B out of the closet of fiction/poetry and making of it a viable contemporary prose—especially when the innovative fiction writers in the post-World War II period, writers like Barth, Barthelme, Brauti-

9

gan, Burroughs, and others, developed Grammar B into a full-fledged and
enduring kind of writing, with a full display of its capacities and possibilities
in a remarkable number of stories, novels, plays, and even poetry.

The precedent of using Grammar B in prose and the grand demonstrations of Grammar B in latter-day fiction/poetry coalesced in the
emergence of the "new journalism," and if any single event can be identified
as establishing Grammar B as a truly significant alternative in our time it is
Tom Wolfe's writing his now-famous essay (for *Esquire* magazine, 1964) and
book (1965): *The Kandy-Colored Tangerine-Flake Streamline Baby*. According
to Wolfe's own account, he went to California for *Esquire* to do a story on
custom cars; having studied the California car-culture, he returned to New
York and sat down to write his copy. He "had a lot of trouble analyzing
exactly what I had on my hands." (Note the key word "analyzing" which has
to do with the traditional grammar of style.) Finally up against a deadline, the
only thing Wolf could do was to "type up my notes" with the understanding
that the *Esquire* editor "will get somebody else to write" the story. About
eight in the evening, Wolfe started typing his notes in the form of a
memorandum: "I just started recording it all, and inside a couple of hours,
typing along like a madman, I could tell that something was beginning to
happen. By midnight this memorandum was . . . twenty pages long and I was
still typing like a maniac. About 2 A.M. . . . I turned on WABC, a radio
station that plays rock and roll music all night, and got a little more manic. I
wrapped up the memorandum about 6:15 A.M. and by this time it was 49 pages
long. I took it over to *Esquire* as soon as they opened about 9:30 A.M." (Note
Wolfe's "madman" and "manic" and references—words that should not be
read pejoratively at all, but as attempts simply to describe something contrary
to analysis and order.)

Esquire published it as written and thus "new journalism" was introduced
into contemporary culture and thus, too, Grammar B made one of its most
dramatic appearances in contemporary/popular prose style: a grammar of style
that could tolerate the quasi-amorphousness of a memo, the ongoing chain
effect of thought-association, the incorporation of notes directly into a text.
Wolfe had liberated himself and, according to Michael L. Johnson in *The
New Journalism*, "found himself outside what he calls the old 'system of ideas,'
the old journalistic conceptions of style, and the old clichés concerning what
deserves the journalist's attention. . . ."

Listening to Wolfe's account, we have to take notice, of course, of the
part that twentieth-century electronic media have played in bringing the
alternate style on stage. Wolfe's listening to rock and roll music on radio was
but a minor incident so far as his own composition was concerned, yet the
influence of radio, television, and movies on the evolution of Grammar B is
tremendously important. Many of the stylistic devices that finally became a
part of Grammar B are based on cinematic techniques as well as on the audio
techniques found in radio and stereo systems. More important, it was the

electronic media that used an alternate style so frequently and so powerfully that its grammar could no longer be ignored; especially the movie—emerging as the most exciting art form of the century—revealed the alternate grammar of style in such spectacular and acceptable ways to such sizeable audiences that Anglo-American culture in the sixties and seventies was prepared to be hospitable when the same grammar of style flowered in written composition.

The alternate style has received a certain amount of describing and evaluating in recent times, mainly by literary critics, though no real codification of the style has taken place. (You can't buy a textbook anywhere that will show you how to write a theme in Grammar B.) Most discussions are still tentative attempts to define the "grammar," to indicate the general boundaries of it, to suggest its general characteristics. In the *New York Times Book Review*, Roger Shattuck discussed, in his review of Donald Barthelme's *The Dead Father* (November 9, 1975), the characteristics of a certain way of writing that he acknowledges runs all the way from Sterne's *Tristram Shandy* through Baudelaire's prose poems, to such recent novels as Paul Metcalf's *Genos*, Guy Davenport's *Tatlin!*, Alain Robbe-Grillet's *In the Labyrinth*, and Thomas Pynchon's *Gravity's Rainbow*. Though Shattuck, rather typically of current commentators, limited his discussion to works of fiction, he nevertheless was dealing with the alternate grammar of style which, according to his analysis, is characterized by four basic techniques: montage, pastiche, linguistic generation (that is, a great deal of word play and linguistic manipulation) and supersaturation (that is, a great amount of verbosity, repetition, restatement).

Shattuck's very brief and limited list of characteristics is, nevertheless, a sign of a growing attempt in American literature/writing to codify the alternate style, to say just exactly how it does work. And behind the attempt at codification is perhaps the recognition of the alternate style as having validity as an equal partner in composition in general. Admittedly, Shattuck asks the questions, "Who let all these winds of change out of the bag? . . . Can he so easily jettison the myth of organic unity?" And the questions imply skepticism and some anxiety. Yet behind the questions is perhaps the recognition that the alternate style is not going away.

And why won't it go away? There are two major justifications for the alternate style, justifications for its emergence and endurance over the past two centuries and for its particular validity here in the final decades of the twentieth century. First of all, there is a general cultural value, so we increasingly realize, in having access to "both sides of the coin" in all our affairs, to having access—in life styles or literary styles—to what William Blake labeled the "contraries." The "contrary" or "alternate" completes a picture, saves us from the absoluteness of one single style, provides us with the stimulating, illuminating, and refreshing *opposite* that makes the traditional grammar of style even more meaningful and useful: as the alternate grammar of style more and more takes on strong and viable identity, so the traditional style is lifted from the lethargy/monotony of its solitude. There is, indeed, a certain "through the looking glass" quality to the alternate style, but that very quality reminds us, in composition as in life, that wholeness must embrace all possibilities; that true expertise in writing must always be able to evaluate one writing procedure in the context provided by a totally different writing procedure.

Second, the alternate style is justified today because it is seen by many writers as a more appropriate grammar so far as the communication of certain realities is concerned. Many writers believe that there are things to say, not only in fiction but in nonfiction as well, that simply cannot be effectively communicated via a traditional style; that there are things to say in a highly technological, electronic, socially complex, politically and spiritually confused era that simply cannot be reflectecd in language if language is limited to the traditional style; that the "conventions" of language in the traditional style are so much a product of certain thought processes, certain world views, certain notions about the nature of man and society that the conventions force upon much of our content a compromise, a qualification, an unwanted prevarication. Whether or not "style" can ever "match" reality is a debatable question, of course; but if the illusion can be maintained by rhetoricians and stylists that the traditional style somehow matches and corresponds to an orderly universe or an orderly mentality, then surely a similar illusion can be posited that a variegated, discontinuous, fragmented grammar of style corresponds to an amorphous and inexplicable universe and mentality. More important than whether such a correspondence is "true" is the fact that it can be taught and maintained as a writing convention; a mixed metaphor may not really correspond to a mixed world, but if we agree on it, then it does: the mixed metaphor becomes a "word" in our stylistic vocabulary, the definition of which is "mixed-upness"—mixed-up societies, personalities, cultures, and what have you.

One of the most vigorous justifications of the alternate grammar of style on grounds of better correspondence with reality is that given by Jerome Klinkowitz and John Somer in their introduction to *Innovative Fiction* (New York: Dell, 1972). Though talking only about fiction, their argument applies finally to all kinds of writing: "The reorganization of values in the twentieth century has displaced man from his traditional notion of self. To regain any notion of the self at all, new writers . . . have placed themselves at the fore of movements to understand and artistically interpret the Einsteinian, relativistic, fourth-dimensional world, and the quality of man's life in it."

Or consider George Steiner's warning in *After Babel*: "In certain civilizations there come epochs in which syntax stiffens, in which the available resources of live perception and restatement wither. . . . Instead of acting as a living membrane, grammar and vocabulary become a barrier to new feeling. A civilization is imprisoned in a linguistic contour which no longer matches, or matches only at certain ritual, arbitrary points, the changing landscape of fact."

Or simply consider the obvious: Language, by the very nature of its users, is linear—a one-word-after-another phenomenon. But human perceptions are not that linear at all.

Other justifications for the alternate style can perhaps be found. (Perhaps it is justifiable on the grounds of novelty or welcome relief if nothing else.) But the justification of "wholeness through inclusion of the alternate" and "better correspondence with certain aspects of reality" have been enough to support the alternate style and give writers enough reason to push its grammar beyond experimentation and give it the status of utility.

3

The writer who wishes to practice the alternate style—for whatever reasons—will want to master a number of stylistic maneuvers and conventions (the "grammar") from which she may select the particular devices/schemes/techniques that seem useful in a particular communication/rhetorical situation and that she can combine in a manner appropriate, as she so judges, to the composition she is writing. The following presentation of such maneuvers/conventions/devices is not complete, of course, but is representative of the sort of writing practices found in the alternate grammar of style and does provide a writer with a basic and beginning set of "things to do":

The Crot. A crot is an obsolete word meaning "bit" or "fragment." The term was given new life by Tom Wolfe in his "Introduction" to a collection of *Esquire* magazine fiction, *The Secret Life of Our Times,* edited by Gordon Lish (New York: Doubleday, 1973). A basic element in the alternate grammar of style, and comparable somewhat to the stanza in poetry, the crot may range in length from one sentence to twenty or thirty sentences. It is fundamentally an autonomous unit, characterized by the absence of any transitional devices that might relate it to preceding or subsequent crots and, because of this independent and discrete nature of crots, they create a general effect of metastasis—using that term from classical rhetoric to label, as Fritz Senn suggests in the *James Joyce Quarterly* (Summer, 1975), any "rapid transition from one point of view to another." In its most intense form, it is characterized by a certain abruptness in its termination: "As each crot breaks off," Tom Wolfe says, "it tends to make one's mind search for some point that must have just been made—*presque vu!*—almost seen! In the hands of a writer who really understands the device, it will have you making crazy leaps of logic, leaps you never dreamed of before."

The provenance of the crot may well be in the writer's "note" itself—in the research note, in the sentence or two one jots down to record a moment or an idea or to describe a person or place. The crot is essentially the note left free of verbal ties with other surrounding notes.

Very brief crots have the quality of an aphorism or proverb, while longer crots may have the quality of descriptive or narrative passages found in the traditional grammar of style. The crots, of whatever kind, may be presented in nearly random sequence or in sequences that finally suggest circularity. Rarely is any stronger sense of order (such as would be characteristic of traditional style) imposed on them—though the absence of traditional order is far more pronounced when the device is used in fiction and poetry. The general idea of unrelatedness present in crot writing suggests correspondence—for those who seek it—with the fragmentation and even egalitarianism of contemporary experience, wherein the events, personalities, places of life have no particular superior or inferior status to dictate priorities of presentation.

Nearly always crots are separated one from the other by white space, and at times each crot is given a number or, on rare occasion, a title. That little spectrum—white space only, white space plus a numbering, white space plus a titling—provides a writer with a way of indicating an increase in separation, discreteness, isolation. Occasionally, but rarely, crots are not separated one from the other typographically but the reader is left to discover the "separation" while he seems to be reading a linear, continuous text; jamming crots against each other becomes a fourth option in presentation, one that provides a greater sense of surprise (or perhaps bewilderment) for the reader.

The effect of writing in crots is intensified, or course, as the number increases. Since each crot is not unlike a snapshot or a color slide, the overall composition, using crots, is similar to a slide show, especially if the slides have not been arranged into any neat and tidy sequence. "My Trip to New Orleans" written in traditional style will have some sort of orderly quality to it: the trip will be presented chronologically, spatially, or what have you. But "My Trip to New Orleans," written in the alternate style, will depend, not on the order in which the "slides" appear, but on the sharp, exceptional quality of each crot or slide and on the "crazy leaps of logic" that Wolfe mentioned, with the reader jolted from one snapshot to the next, frequently surprised to be given an "aerial view of New Orleans as the plane begins its descent to the airport" and immediately after that "a close-up of an antique candelabrum used in a Louisiana antebellum mansion and now on sale in a New Orleans antique store" followed by "a broad shot of Canal Street" followed by a picture of "Marge and Myrtle getting into the taxicab at the airport to come into the city."

Crots at their best will not be all that banal, of course, in content, but will have some sharp, arresting, or provocative quality to them. Even if they are unable to stand alone as minicompositions (sometimes they actually are capable of that) and gain their full effect in association with others, each one should have a certain integrity and interestingness about it. Crots may be written in any dictional style deemed appropriate to the communication occasion, with a single dictional style prevailing, usually, throughout an entire composition. On rare occasions, dictional level may shift from one crot to another, but usually the level of diction is a constant.

Crots are akin, obviously, to a more general kind of "block" writing—the kind of writing found, for instance, in E. M. Forster's "The Last Parade" and in Katherine Anne Porter's essay, "Audubon's Happy Land." In such block writing, the authors have strung together short, fairly discrete units of composition to make whole compositions. Likewise, a series of crots is not unlike a collection of aphorisms—say those of Eric Hoffer who, in a book like *The Passionate State of Mind and Other Aphorisms,* has brought together brief compositional units, some a sentence long, some several paragraphs long, each quite distinct from the other, yet grouped into a whole composition on the basis of a certain attitude and view of life common to them all. These compositions of blocks or aphorisms are so much in the spirit of crot writing that they may be considered a part of its development out of a traditional grammar of style into the alternate grammar. The writing of Forster, Porter, and Hoffer—in prose *and* nonfiction—gives evidence of the usefulness of something other than the ordered, linear procedure of traditional style even to writers who would not be identified as especially experimental or stylistically daring.

Likewise, the question-and-answer format—not particularly daring in itself—tends to support nonlinear crot writing: questions and answers (frequently presented as mock-interview) become a way of presenting information, ideas, data in segments, more discrete, needing less transition, than ordinary linear discourse could tolerate.

The Labyrinthine Sentence and the Sentence Fragment. Though the alternate grammar of style uses the ordinary range of sentence types, it makes use also, and more frequently, of two radical sentence types: the labyrinthine sentence and the sentence fragment. And it tolerates a certain mixture of sentence types that would not be found in the traditional grammar of style. The alternate style tolerates great leaps from the long, labyrinthine sentence to the short fragmentary sentence, creating a sharp, startling effect at times. Yet it is not committed entirely to the startling juxtaposing: often enough a composition in the alternate style will be wholly labyrinthine or wholly fragmentary. Or at times, a most ordinary traditional sentence style will prevail. Usually, if traditional sentence types are to be mixed with the more radical forms, the mix will involve only traditional types and sentence fragments. Rarely do the traditional sentences and labyrinthine sentence mix successfully.

The labyrinthine sentence in particular is a long complex sentence, with a certain "endless" quality to it, full of convolutions, marked by appositives, parentheses, digressions. A parody through exaggeration of the highly structured Johnsonian sentence of the eighteenth century, the labyrinthine has immediate ancestry in the long, radical sentences of twentieth-century fiction—such as the famous Molly Bloom one-sentence soliloquy that ends Joyce's *Ulysses*. One current master of the labyrinthine sentence is William Gass; to wit, the opening sentence from *On Being Blue*—

> Blue pencils, blue noses, blue movies, laws, blue legs and stockings, the language of birds, bees, and flowers as sung by longshoremen, that lead-like look the skin has when affected by cold, contusion, sickness, fear; the rotten rum or gin they call blue ruin and the blue devils of its delirium; Russian cats and oysters, a withheld or imprisoned breath, the blue they say that diamonds have, deep holes in the ocean and the blazers which English athletes earn that gentlemen may wear; afflictions of the spirit—dumps, mopes, Mondays—all that's dismal—low-down gloomy music, Nova Scotians, cyanosis, hair rinse, bluing, bleach; the rare blue dahlia like that blue moon shrewd things happen only once in, or the call for trumps in whist (but who remembers whist or what the death of unplayed games is like?), and correspondingly the flag, Blue Peter, which is our signal for getting under way; a swift pitch, Confederate money, the shaded slopes of clouds and mountains, and so the constantly increasing absentness of Heaven (*ins Blaue hinein,* the Germans say), consequently the color of everything that's empty: blue bottles, bank accounts, and compliments, for instance, or, when the sky's turned turtle, the blue-green bleat of ocean (both the same), and, when in Hell, its neatly landscaped rows of concrete huts and gas-blue flames; social registers, examination booklets, blue bloods, balls, and bonnets, beards, coats, collars, chips, and cheese . . . the pedantic, indecent and censorious . . . watered twilight, sour sea: through a scrambling of accidents, blue has become their color, just as it's stood for fidelity.

Or this labyrinthine sentence used by Gass in an article entitled "Ein Gott vermage," which deals with Rilke translations and which appeared in *American Poetry Review* (March/April, 1978):

> Who has not heard it? elaborately how, near ruins where Dante also had composed, that rootless poet whom we've followed for so long like a stray we know the smell of his heels, a wanderer who always brings us strangely home, Rainer Maria Rilke, imprisoned by a bitter Adriatic winter and more willingly by the stones of the place itself—deserted by the Muses too, barren, dry of spirit; who has not felt it? painfully how he had been driven deeply into himself like a stake, stretched to onion thin transparency wherever he reached by a loneliness which had for months embarrassed his much prized solitude with occult visitations and hand-made sex—shameful and humiliating, sterile as a wooden cuckoo; who has not

read it? repeatedly how he was distracted on this fateful morning by an annoying business letter he felt asked too loudly for its answer—with sound and sense absorbed, he became an echo, rattle in a hollow gourd; and while working who has not often remembered it? reverently how the poet was walking then along the precipitous pale edge of the Duino Castle cliffs, head bent into a bright wind which buried his breath, when he heard, as if from the wind itself, the celebrated question with which the *Elegies* were at last to announce themselves: *Wer, wenn. ich schriee, hörte mich denn aus der Engle Ordnungen?*

And there are numerous other practitioners. One interesting (and perhaps unlikely) example that comes to mind is the long opening periodic sentence of *Rousseau and Revolution* by Will and Ariel Durant.

How did it come about that a man born poor, losing his mother at birth and soon deserted by his father, afflicted with a painful and humiliating disease, left to wander for twelve years among alien cities and conflicting faiths, repudiated by society and civilization, repudiating Voltaire, Diderot, the *Encyclopédie*, and the Age of Reason, driven from place to place as a dangerous rebel, suspected of crime and insanity, and seeing, in his last months, the apotheosis of his greatest enemy—how did it come about that this man, after his death, triumphed over Voltaire, revived religion, transformed education, elevated the morals of France, inspired the Romantic movement and the French Revolution, influenced the philosophy of Kant and Schopenhauer, the plays of Schiller, the novels of Goethe, the poems of Wordsworth, Byron, and Shelley, the socialism of Marx, the ethics of Tolstoi, and, altogether, had more effect upon posterity than any other writer or thinker of that eighteenth century in which writers were more influential than they had ever been before?

The long, almost picaresque sentence—through which an author rides picaro-like—works for many writers as a correspondence to the complexity, confusion, even sheer talkativeness of modern society. When a writer talks about Walt Whitman this way—

Walt Whitman, born on Paumanok (that is: Long Island), saw in that island's shape (understandably, when you look at the map) the fish that, in the context of Western-Christian iconography, equals Christ equals rebirth equals, especially for Whitman, messianic connotations and (given Whitman's translation of biographical events and conditions into transcendental mythological patterns) therefore portends for "I, Walt

Whitman" (to be born later, again, with the writing of *Leaves of Grass*) a divine dimension and a capacity for illuminating the masses who, though they never read him, remained always his projected audience, and revealing, to the enslaved (more than "the slaves," of course; all of us at one time or another) a certain kind of liberation, freedom, escape from the prison.

—he is suggesting, via style, the entangling environment in which the masses and the enslaved are living and from which Whitman sought to rescue them.

In contrast with this kind of labyrinthine sentence but often its companion (a la Quixote and Panza), the sentence fragment—frequently a single word or a very short phrase of only two or three words—suggests a far greater awareness of separation and fragmentation: not entanglement but isolation. It is also a highly emphatic kind of sentence and, in conjunction with other sentence types, creates a variegated, more sharply pointed kind of reading line. Gertrude Stein was a great pioneer in the use of the single word/word phrase/sentence fragment unit. As Robert Bartlett Haas says in an introductory note to Stein's essay on "Grant or Rutherford B. Hayes" in *How Writing Is Written:*

> During the late 1920's and early 1930's, Gertrude Stein seems to have been dealing with . . . what the sentence was . . . as seen from the standpoint of an American syntax. Another concern was the description of events by portraying movement so intense as to be a thing in itself, not a thing in relation to something else.
>
> "Grant or Rutherford B. Hayes" attempts to do this by replacing the noun and the adjective and emphasizing the more active parts of speech. Here a driving pulse is created by syncopating the sentence. The thrust comes from a concentrated use of verbs and verb phrases.

Only a few words from Stein's essay are needed to indicate her method:

Grant or Rutherford B. Hayes.
Jump. Once for all. With the praising of. Once for all.
As a chance. To win.
Once for all. With a. Chance. To win.

The farther reach of sentence types in the alternate grammar of style provides the writer with a much greater number of options. He can write the crots of the alternate grammar (a) in the traditional sentence types, (b) in the labyrinthine sentence, (c) in sentence fragments, or (d) in combinations of (i.) traditional sentences and sentence fragments or (ii.) labyrinthine sentences and sentence fragments.

The List. To create a list, a writer presents a series of items, usually removed from sentence structure or at least very independent of such structure. Usually a list contains a minimum of five items, the items being related in subject matter but presented in list form to avoid indicating any other relationship among the items than that they are *all there at once,* that they are parts of the whole. Presenting a list of items is comparable to presenting a "still life" of objects without indication of foreground or background, without any indication of relative importance, without any suggestion at all of cause-effect, this-before-that, rank, or the like. Obviously the items on the list must be presented one first, one second, one third—but the sequence is generally arbitrary and meaningless.

Here is a list from F. Scott Fitzgerald's *The Crack-Up:*

Seen in a Junk Yard. Dogs, chickens with few claws, brass fittings, T's elbow, rust everywhere, bales of metal 1800 lbs, plumbing fixtures, bathtubs, sinks, water pumps, wheels, Fordson tractor, acetylene lamps for tractors, sewing machine, bell on dinghy, box of bolts (No. 1), van, stove, auto stuff (No. 2), army trucks, cast iron body, hot dog stand, dinky engines, sprockets like watch parts, hinge all taken apart on building side, motorcycle radiators, George on the high army truck.

Here is another from D. H. Lawrence's essay, "Fenimore Cooper's Leatherstocking Novels":

Two monsters loomed on Cooper's horizon.
    Mrs. Cooper   My Work
    My Work   My Wife
    My Wife   My Work
        The Dear Children
           My Work!!!
There you have the essential keyboard of Cooper's soul.

Adapted from the plethora series found in traditional grammar of style, and antedated by "catalogues" such as appear in Whitman's poetry, the list stands in stark simplicity—a list of objects, observations, or what have you—to give a quick representation of a character, a situation, a place by the simple device of selecting items to represent the subject under discussion. Donald Barthelme, a frequent user of lists, can range—as he does in a short story, "City Life"—from a list dealing with television viewing—

On 7 there's "Johnny Allegro" with George Raft and Nina Foch. On 9 "Johnny Angel" with George Raft and Claire Trevor. On 11 there's "Johnny Apollo" with Tyrone Power and Dorothy Lamour. On 13 is "Johnny Concho" with Frank Sinatra and Phyllis Kirk. On 2 is "Johnny Dark" with Tony Curtis and Piper Laurie. On 4 is "Johnny Eager" with Robert Taylor and Lana Turner. On 5 is "Johnny O'Clock" with Dick Powell and Evelyn Keyes. On 31 is "Johnny Trouble" with Stuart Whitman and Ethel Barrymore.

—to a "list" description of a wedding:

Elsa and Jaces bombarded with flowers
Fathers and mothers riding on the city railway
The minister raises his hand
Evacuation of the sacristy: bomb threat
Black limousines with ribbons tied to their aerials
Several men on balconies who appear to be signaling, or applauding
Traffic lights
Pieces of blue cake
Champagne

Though lists may be presented in a straight reading line, they are usually presented in columnar form, the items arranged typographically one beneath the other just as one writes a grocery list.

Consider, for instance, this "poem" by Joshua Norton in *The Blue and the Gray*. The poem is entitled "Play Stage" and is a list in the purest sense:

Saturday
Shrank
September
Past
Eternity
Extended
Weather
Wrapped
Undershirt & Sweater
Unfolded
Stage & Show
Linked
Day
Make-Shift
Blueprint

Street & Block
Main-line
Suburb
Stream & Breeze
Limbo
Childhood
Danced . . .
Performance
Squirrel
Dead
Fluid
Vapor
Lit
Lighter
Flame
Kindled
Curled
Smoke
Vision
Placed
Puzzle (yellow line)
Play
Cremation . . .

Curtain
Drawn.

One of the attractions of the list to the contemporary writer is that—disregarding the fact that bias may have entered into the selection of the items in the first place—the list is basically a presentation of items without commentary, seeming to say, "Consider these items without any help from the writer. The writer is keeping her mouth shut. She is simply giving you the data, the evidence, the facts, the objects. You, the reader, must add them up and evaluate them." Or there is the suggestion that there are no "values" at all that can be imposed upon the list, that reality stands before us neutral, amoral, and that if we do impose values upon a list it is an arbitrary act on our part.

Whereas in the traditional grammar of style, one might write—

Whitman grew up as a boy on Long Island, absorbing all the images of sea and sky and shore, all the images of the pastoral world that were always to be a part of his poetry even as he later celebrated the urban glories of Manhattan.

—in the alternate style one might well write—

Whitman grew up as a boy on Long Island.
    Sea.
    Gulls.
    Sky.
    Shore.
    Stones.
    Roses.
    Salt air.
    Tides.
    Farms.
    Dusty Roads.
    Mockingbirds.
    Horses.
    Summer Clouds.
Later: Brooklyn. Later: Manhattan. But always: Sea. Stones. Cattle. Birds. Lilacs. Even as the metropolis paved its way toward mercantile grandeur and urban glory.

The difference between the two is not a matter of "quality," but is a matter of differing effects, differing reader involvement, differing authorial voice. One is no more creative than the other; one is no more fictional than the other.

The value of the list as a stylistic instrument is given one of its most entertaining celebrations by Guillermo Cabrera Infante in a September 19, 1977 *New Yorker* article? essay? story? entitled "Revelations of a List-Maker." Infante points out that

> The finest pages of this century's Fitzgerald are filled with names, in a list, of guests at anticlimactic parties. Hemingway, for his part, recommended that beginning writers study the racing bulletin—the best advice that this linear writer could ever have given. Auden, a born list-maker, spoke up not only for railway timetables but for "every kind of list."
>
> More seriously, or perhaps less timidly (or, if my enemies prefer it, more incoherently), I am planning to write a masterwork, no less, which will consist of nothing but a list.

Double-Voice. Even in nonfiction, as in fiction, a writer speaks with a "voice"—if not always the same voice in all his writing, certainly a given voice in a given composition. Indeed, the creation of "voice" is one of the tasks of style, and the traditional grammar of style has always been used for that purpose among others. In the alternate style, however, voice is not always considered a singular characteristic, but often enough a plural characteristic—not a surprising consideration in an age of stereophonics and multi-media dispositions in general.

Writers use double-voice many times when they feel that they could say this *or* that about a subject; when they feel that two attitudes toward a subject are equally valid; when they wish to suggest that there are two sides to the story (whatever the story may be); when they wish to distinguish between their roles as (a) provider of information and data, and (b) commentator upon information and data; or when they wish to effect a style corresponding to ambiguous realities.

The double-voice may be presented in straight-line form:

Whitman was born on Long Island in 1819. Are island children marked for a certain sense of individuality, or separation? He was the Whitman's second child. Do "second" children make a greater struggle for identity than the oldest or the youngest? Whitman moved with his parents to Brooklyn when he was four years old. Have children, by the age of four, absorbed most of their primary images, established their essential attitudes and feelings toward life regardless where they move?

Straight-line presentation of double-voice is what John Barth uses, for instance, in "Lost in the Funhouse." One example occurs in the opening paragraph of the story:

For whom is the funhouse fun? Perhaps for lovers. For Ambrose it is a *place of fear and confusion.* He has come to the seashore with his family for the holiday, the *occasion of their visit is Independence Day, the most important secular holiday of the United States of America.* A single straight underline is the manuscript mark for italic type, *which in turn* is the printed equivalent to oral emphasis of words and phrases as well as the customary type for titles of complete works, not to mention. Italics are also employed, in fiction stories especially, for "outside," intrusive, or artificial voices, such as radio announcements, the texts of telegrams and newspaper articles, et cetera. They should be used *sparingly.* If passages originally in roman type are italicized by someone repeating them, it's customary to acknowledge the fact. *Italics mine.*

The shift of voice that comes with the words "A single straight underline" provides Barth with a way of writing both as storyteller and as "observer" of the storyteller.

Obviously, one effective way for writers to present double-voice is to present parallel passages in column form, simply running two tracks of composition down the page, side by side. John Cage does this often enough, notably in his essay on "Erik Satie," in *Silence*. In this 1958 essay, Cage alternates two voices, one indicated by italics to the left of the page, the other by roman type to the right of the page:

There'll probably be some music, but we'll manage to find a quiet corner where we can talk.

A few days ago it rained. I should be out gathering mushrooms. But here I am, having to write about Satie. In an unguarded moment I said I would. Now I am pestered with a deadline. Why, in heaven's name, don't people read the books about him that are available, play the music that's published? Then I for one could go back to the woods and spend my time profitably.

Nevertheless, we must bring about a music which is like furniture—a music, that is, which will be part of the noises of the environment, will take them into consideration. I think of it as melodious, softening the noises of the knives and forks, not dominating them, not imposing itself. It would fill up those heavy silences that sometimes fall between friends dining together. It would spare them the trouble of paying attention to their own banal remarks. And at the same time it would neutralize the street noises which so indiscretely enter into the play of conversation. To make such music would be to respond to a need.

Records, too, are available. But it would be an act of charity even to oneself to smash them whenever they are discovered. They are useless except for that and for the royalties which the composer, dead now some thirty-odd years, can no longer pick up.

We cannot doubt that animals both love and practice music. That is evident. But it seems their musical system differs from ours. It is another school. . . . We are not familiar with their didactic works. Perhaps they don't have any.

In another essay, "Where Are We Going? And What Are We Doing?" Cage sets up double-voice, at times even triple-voice, by writing this way—

If we set out to catalogue things
•
•
•
today, we find ourselves rather
•
•
•
endlessly involved in cross-
•
•
•
referencing. Would it not be
Those of us who don't agree are going
•
•
•
less efficient to start the other
around together. The string Duchamp
dropped.
•
•
•
go to all the parties, ending up
been found dangerous for them to
•
•

way around, after the fashion of
He took the apartment without being
able to
•
some obscure second-hand
bookstore?
pay for it. They danced on a concrete
floor.
•
•
The candles at the Candlelight
Concert are
•
One New Year's Eve I had too
electric. It was found dangerous
•
•
•
many invitations. I decided to
for them to be wax. It has not yet
•
•
•
could scarcely put it down. It is
absolutely
•
•

at the most interesting one. I	**charming. I'm going to write to the**
•	**author.**
be electric—and this in spite of	How can we go over there when

and so forth.

By far, though, the standard way of presenting double-voice is simply to present the columns without any further complications:

Whitman was born in 1819 on Long Island. When he was four, his parents moved to Brooklyn where Whitman grew up and went to school. All his youth he spent, one place or another, in town or in country, betwixt East River and the Atlantic Ocean.	We are born by accident in a certain location, yet the location impinges upon our soul and psyche, and we absorb the shapes and sounds and sights peculiar to that location and our view of reality is constructed from this primary, childhood material.

And obviously, two *lists* can run parallel to each other—doing all that lists themselves do and at the same time creating the double-voice:

Sea	Atlantic/Womb & Tomb/Such Mystery
Gulls	Arcs of whiteness/plaintive screams
Sky	Endless/one should not stare into space too long a time
Shore	Boundaries/the line between
Stones	Foundation & Crushing Force
Roses	Perfume & Thorn
Salt Air	Wake me up! Sting against my face!
Tides	Of blood
Farms	Pastoral themes/dirty labor in barns
Country Roads	Delicate tracks/muddy ruts
Mockingbirds	Music & Irony
Horses	I stare into their eyes & wonder about the universe.
Summer Clouds	Like every child, I Walt Whitman, lie & stare into their magic shapes, their shifting forms, and see men and beasts.

(Double-voice embraces, actually, what might be called double-perspective or double-thought, and it is sometimes difficult to distinguish between a dual vision and a dual sound. Many times the writer, in juxtaposing two statements, gives less attention to distinguishing his "voices" and concentrates on the fact that he is seeing two scenes at once or is approaching a subject from two different angles at once.)

Repetitions/Repetends/Refrains. Repetitions play a more important part in the alternate style than they do in the traditional; repetitions are used to achieve a kind of momentum in composition when traditional continuity has been supressed, eliminated, or handled with such subtlety that it scarcely seems present at all. The repetitions come in all forms: simple *repetitions* of individual words; phrases and sentences used as *refrains;* words, phrases, or sentences used as *repetends.* The repetitions are mostly devoted to binding and holding together, creating even at times a certain rhythm that carries a reader through disjointed sentences and passages. Perhaps the concern with repetitions in the alternate style is compensatory for a pervasive acceptance of fragmentation and discontinuity.

In the recent volume, *Style and Text* (ed. Hakan Ringbom, issued by the Abö Akademie, Finland), Irma Ranavaara notes, in her essay on Virginia Woolf's style, that Woolf made great use of repetition, a use that ranges through all parts of speech. Some examples given by Professor Ranavaara are these, taken from Woolf's last novel, *Between the Acts:*

> She had come into the stable yard where the dogs were chained; where the buckets stood; where the great pear tree spread its ladder of branches against the wall.

> What a cackle, what a raggle, what a yaffle—as they call the woodpecker, the laughing bird that flits from tree to tree.

> Faster, faster, faster, it whizzed, whirred, buzzed.

> The cook's hands cut, cut, cut.

Woolf was concerned in all her writing, of course, with answering the question, "How can we combine the old words in new orders so they survive, so that they create beauty, so that they tell the truth?" And she foraged into the alternate grammar of style, trying this and trying that, with repetition being one of the stylistic devices she used heavily to escape the very economy of the traditional style and all the implications of that economy.

Woolf's repetitions, though of high incidence, are essentially limited to an easily achieved epizeuxis. As D. H. Lawrence's repetitions frequently are, though he—more than Woolf—presses repetition to extraordinary lengths (as in this passage from "Herman Melville's *Moby Dick*"):

Doom.

Doom! Doom! Doom! Something seems to whisper it in the very dark trees of America. Doom!

Doom of what?

Doom of our white day. We are doomed, doomed. And the doom is in America. The doom of our white day.

Ah, well, if my day is doomed, and I am doomed with my day, it is something greater than I which dooms me, so I accept my doom as a sign of the greatness which is more than I am.

Melville knew. He knew his race was doomed. His white soul, doomed. His great white epoch, doomed. Himself, doomed. The idealist, doomed. The spirit, doomed.

Gertrude Stein, in such an essay as "American Food and American Houses" (1938), uses a slightly more subtle kind of repetition and in ways more typical of the alternate grammar. Stein writes such sentences as "Salads fruit salads have immensely taken their place," with the "salad" repetition being quite different from ordinary epizeuxis. Likewise, her repetition of the word "pancake" in this sentence:

Then there used to be so many kinds of pancakes, every kind of pancake, that too has disappeared the pancake has pretty well disappeared and I imagine that there are lots of little Americans who have never even heard of them never even heard of the word pancakes. (Haas, *op cit.*)

The efforts of a Stein or a Lawrence or a Woolf are simply preludes to the full use of repetition that we find in full-blown examples of the alternate style. When we come to Tom Wolfe's essay "Las Vegas (What?) Las Vegas (Can't Hear You! Too Noisy! Las Vegas!!!" we find him opening with a tremendously exaggerated super-epizeuxis, repeating the word "Hernia" thirty times in a row; then—after a slight interruption for the phrase "eight is the point, the point is eight"—repeating the word "hernia" another seven times, pausing slightly for the phrase "all right" and repeating "hernia" another four times, pausing again for the phrase "hard eight," then finishing out the opening paragraph with another sixteen "hernias."

Hernia, hernia, hernia, hernia, hernia, hernia, hernia, hernia, hernia, hernia, hernia, hernia, hernia, HERNia; hernia, HERNia, hernia, hernia, hernia, hernia, HERNia, HERNia, HERNia, hernia, hernia, hernia, hernia, hernia, hernia, hernia, eight is the point, the point is eight; hernia hernia, HERNia; hernia hernia, hernia, hernia, all right, hernia, hernia, hernia, hernia, hard eight, hernia, hernia, hernia, HERNia,

hernia, hernia, hernia, HERNia, hernia, hernia, hernia, HERNia, her-
nia, hernia, hernia, hernia

Wolfe's repetition in this case suggests movement and energy, and probably most repetitions, when presented in tightly concetrated form this way,
are corresponding to a certain "throb of life." Sometimes, though, repetitions
are less concentrated, more scattered—as in this passage from John Dos
Passos's *U.S.A.*:

> Thomas A. Edison at eighty-two worked sixteen hours a day; he never
> worried about mathematics or the social system or generalized
> philosophical concepts;
>   in collaboration with Henry Ford and Harvey Firestone who never
> worried about mathematics or the social system or generalized
> philosophical concepts;
>   he worked sixteen hours a day trying to find a substitute for rubber;
> whenever he read about anything he tried it out; whenever he got a
> hunch he went to the laboratory and tried it out.

In such repetition the correspondence is probably more with the idea of
inevitable recurrence of experience, the "sameness" and "inevitability" of
reality, a recognition that in reality there are both stabilizing "things we
count on" and boring things that never go away. Different writers will find
different values in the repetition peculiar to the alternative style, some writers using it sparingly but some writers creating, with it, a great sense of
saturation and density. Once again, the writer has options.

Language Variegation: Orthographic Schemes and the Foreign Word. A frequent characteristic of the alternate style is a pressing against the walls of
ordinary/orthodox vocabulary, a playing with words/word forms to achieve a
special kind of lexical texture—a reading surface that is exciting and rebel-
lious all at once. Language variegation can range, or course, from the subtle
and occasional to the overt and frequent: the variegation can be a delicate
pattern in the background, scarcely noticed, or it can be a thick, dramatic
lexicality in the foreground, almost dominating the composition in which it
occurs.
     The manipulation of word spellings—orthographic schemes—calculated
and controlled respellings as distinguished from thoughtless misspellings—
have always been a part of creative language experience. See Richard A.
Lanham's *A Handlist of Rhetorical Terms* for identification of numerous orthographic schemes bearing their classical Greek and Latin names. (That

which beareth a classical name [good] cannot be all nouveau [bad].) In the traditional grammar of style, these orthographic schemes—and I use the rubric to cover nearly all forms of exceptional word construction, from acronyms to portmanteaus—have always been considered an "error" in spelling or an "error" in taste. Committed to orthodoxies, especially dictionary-recorded orthodoxies, traditional stylists have no room for one's being "betelephoned to death" by a telephone that "rrrrings" all day, or one's being "disdistracted," or one's being a student in a "universylum," or one's feeling very "laaaazy" in the morning, or one's taking a course in "ufology."

The traditional grammar of style cannot really tolerate—it simply has to red pencil—such a line as "Lie blist'ring fore the visitating sun" with "blist'-ring" an example of *syncope*, "fore" an example of *aphaeresis*, and "visitating" an example of *epenthesis*, all traditional orthographic manipulations. Even though the line may come from published literature (*Two Nobel Kinsmen*, Act I, Scene 1), it really is out of place in Grammar A. Just as Chaucer's "As seld I have the chance" is out of place. Or just as the common street expressions, "irregardless" and "finalize," are stylistic no-no's.

In the alternate grammar of style, however, the orthographic scheme becomes a very appropriate and meaningful stylistic instrument. Without trying to identify all the individual spelling/respelling patterns and possibilities, we can easily recognize the presence of orthographic schemes in such a piece of writing as this from James Joyce's *Finnegans Wake*:

> Our cubehouse still rocks as earwitness to the thunder of his arafatas but we hear also through successive ages that shebby choruysh of unkalified muzzlenimiissilehims that would blackguardise the whitestone ever hurtleturtled out of heaven. Stay us wherefore in our search for tight-eousness, O Sustainer, what time we rise and when we take up to tooth-mick and before we lump down upown our leatherbed and in the night and at the fading of the stars! For a nod to the nabir is better than wink to the wabsanti.

This kind of playing with word spellings (known to the Greeks and Romans, practiced in the Renaissance, delightfully demonstrated for the nineteenth century in Lewis Carroll's jabberwocky [Lewis Carroll, that creator of alternate and anti-worlds, a "through the looking glass" grammar of style], and incorporated by James Joyce into the very fabric of his literary text) becomes a valuable stylistic gesture for the alternate stylist for a number of reasons:

(1) It can signal "fun" and "play" to the reader, help articulate the philosophy and presence of *homo ludens* in a work of writing, or can simply "go for laughs." (2) It can communicate the very underlying unorthodox, antiestablishment, revolutionary posture that the writer may wish to expose in style rather than in overt statements. (3) It can contribute to a kind of

literary mimesis. Not only can it be used (as it occasionally is used in traditional style) to "imitate" dialect or uneducated speech/writing, but to imitate a reality that is poorly represented by neat, orthodox spelling and is better represented by the spelling that involves expansion or compression of words—or even rearrangements and distortions: in a discussion of realities that, in the writer's opinion, are "crazy," a text may be well served by "crazy" spellings; realities that are fractured or fragmented may be complemented, if not actually imitated, by the spelling-games. (4) It can actually expedite meaning in certain instances: a new spelling can sometimes open up the semantic aspects of a word in a way that an orthodox and fixed spelling cannot. Example: When an old abandoned railroad bridge across the Arkansas River was recently converted to pedestrian/bicyclist use in Tulsa, someone creatively decided to name the new spruced-up walkway simply "bRRidge"—a word now painted in modern lettering on the structure. The value of "bRRidge" is that (a) it distinguishes this "bRRidge" from other bridges across the Arkansas in the same area, (b) the doubling and capitalizing of the "r" memorializes the bridge's previous railroad use, (c) the lowercase–uppercase mixture and the epenthesis of the added "r" help create a sense of "play" appropriate to a bridge that's part of Tulsa's park and recreational facilities—it's a place to have "fun."

Another example: A recent headline over a newspaper story dealing with Republican party gains in a city where the Democratic party has always been in the majority reads, in part—"Sloooowly gaining"—with the respelling of "slowly" into "sloooowly" an attempt to imitate or suggest the very length of time it is taking the Republicans to increase their registrations.

In the alternate grammar of style, the orthographic schemes are used for these various purposes—and are used to varying degrees of incidence. Sometimes, orthographic schemes are simply scattered through a text, simply joining with all other Grammar B characteristics in achieving alternate style. At other times, orthographic schemes surge up, as they do in Joyce, to become a major, almost dominant characteristic of style.

The "art" of orthographic schemes is never taught to students, of course, since one of the greatest horrors we face, when in the chambers of Grammar A, is that of misspelling. We have difficulty enough in Grammar A achieving "correct" spelling without tempting fate by teaching students the very mechanics of radical and breathtaking respellings. Yet how stylistically exciting it would be if, on the one hand, a student could write a sentence in Grammar A—"She spent, in opulent splendor, her last lonely days in the paradox of happiness and pain"—and on the other hand could write the same sentence in Grammar B—"In opulented splend she spent her lone last daysly in the para, para, para, in the dox, dox, dox of happainness." The sentences would give differing pictures of the elderly lady: in the second she's in greater disarray, more agitated, etc. A student, a writer, might well decide that *that* picture of the lady was the more effective or more truthful—and he would be able to use it if he were composing in the alternate style.

Another contribution to language variegation is the creative use of the *foreign word:* the use of the non-English word, phrase, quotation—ranging from the single instance taken from a single foreign language to a multitude of instances taken from a diversity of languages—the use depending on what degree and patterning of variegation an author wishes to establish within a particular composition. The range can run from the slightest occurrence (a French word here, a German phrase there) to rather heavy incidence (a Latin quotation in one sentence, followed by a French phrase in another sentence, followed by a Greek word in yet another sentence). The range can extend from Whitman's spotty use of French in *Leaves of Grass* to T. S. Eliot's famous multilingual closure of *The Waste Land*. In the last stanza Eliot gives, in quick order, Italian, Latin, French, Renaissance English, Sanskrit—ending with the famous "Shantih   shantih   shantih."

Grammar A, too, makes use of the foreign word—certainly at certain levels of style, in a searching for just the right terminology, making use of a foreign term when there is no convenient English equivalent. But in Grammar B the foreign word does not necessarily serve such clarifying ends. Rather, Grammar B uses the foreign word not to display or exploit erudition but to display multilingualism *per se*—a deliberate "spilling" over and outside the boundaries of English, a gesturing toward a kind of compositional glossolalia: a mixture of play, mockery, and mystery all at once.

Consider this passage from D. H. Lawrence's essay on Melville's *Moby Dick:*

Now what next?
Who knows? *Quien sabe? Quien sabe, senor?*
Neither Spanish or Saxon America has any answer.
The *Pequod* went down. . . .
Boom! as Vachel Lindsay would say.
To use the words of Jesus, It Is Finished.
Consummatum est!
But *Moby Dick* was first published in 1851. If the Great White Whale sank the ship of the Great White Soul in 1851, what's been happening ever since?

And consider these sentences taken from a personal letter E. E. Cummings wrote in October, 1952, to Ezra Pound—a letter in which the whole idea of language variegation is vividly demonstrated with the use of both orthographic schemes and the foreign word:

& right ye were,Ezree meee by, to communiate the Williamsiana which arrived this day,forwarded from nh:& gladdened my spouse&self. . . .
am in good hands here,belonging to 1 "John Finley"; professing Greek, extolling Humanities,&(tactfully not when I'm around;however)praising O'Possumtotheskies. A nice—the JF—fellow. Has already preserved me from well nigh not numerable "social" phenomena:&(this in thine oreille) will,j'espère, make possible a big escape to ny circa Xmas! . . .

Such language variegation can be an extremely useful device for the alternate stylist—especially on those occasions when it seems particularly necessary to startle/provoke readers out of their Grammar A expectations/ responses; to communicate to readers without delay that an "unboxing" and "repackaging" of style is taking place in front of them.

4

Given such stylistic maneuvers and devices as these (there are many more, of course—including the many that are shared with traditional style and including more exceptional devices absolutely beyond the pale of traditional style, e.g., the non sequitur and the mixed metaphor) the contemporary writer can mix and match as his own compositional inclinations and rhetorical commitments determine. He may, in his use of such maneuvers and devices, achieve, as he often does, two stylistic effects quite characteristic of compositions in the alternate style. They are the effects of (a) synchronicity and (b) collage/montage.

Synchronicity. In the traditional grammar of style all "time" considerations are diachronic or chronological. Even the devices of "foreshadowing" and "flashback" are still part of a diachronic conceptualization. In the alternate style, however, there is an acceptance of "all things present in the present moment" with many of the devices already mentioned implying this effect: double-voice implies a certain simultaneity in reality, two things going on at once. Repetitions/repetends/refrains also imply recurrence: certain material occurs in the composition; one reads it and passes on, assuming *those words* to be in the "past" of the composition; but no—we meet the material again; it was not a prisoner of the "past" but is present now, the same as it was, transcending a past/present/future sequence.

If the desire of the writer is to suggest synchronicity, she can indeed make use of double-voice and repetition. She can make use of the double-column list. She can make use of the labyrinthine sentence, especially when it emphasizes circularity (borrowing epanalepsis from the traditional style and making heavy, exaggerated use of it).

Much use is made also of the present tense to achieve synchronicity, since the present tense can equal both the real present and the historical present; without moving from one verb tense to another, synchronicity can be created—as in such a passage as this:

Whitman is crossing the East River on the Brooklyn Ferry. A woman is giving birth on a farm on Long Island on the thirty-first of May. He observes the reflections in the water. Whitman is dying in Camden. Peter Doyle conducts the trolley through the broad streets of Washington and the old man stares out the window, stares at the American people. The woman calls her second child Walter. And crossing on the ferry with him are all types of people, all the diverse faces, all the diverse parts of the American whole. So he walks through Camden. So he walks through Washington, D.C. He climbs up on the trolley and visits with Peter Doyle. He shortens his name to Walt. He tells his mother he is going to cross on the ferry, make his way to Manhattan, he has things to say. Thus Whitman is born on Paumanok, 1819. Thus he is dying, carefully, in the spring of 1892. He is making a kind of journey through the flow of people and across the broad river.

(Note: In synchronicity, use is often made of transitional and relating words—such as "so," "therefore," "thus," "then"—in a kind of "binding of time," parodying the traditional grammar of style wherein transition/relationship is accepted and expected. The resulting non sequiturs are a by-product, yet become an important characteristic of the alternate style, since the non sequiturs cut through old logical patterns and question the validity of old connections.)

Synchronicity is often achieved simply through the scrambling of sentences or paragraphs or crots, scrambling them out of ordinary time sequences, so that one keeps encountering them again and again in a certain time period. For instance, if one had crots dealing with (a) one's arrival in New Orleans, (b) one's visit to the French Quarter, (c) in particular one's dining at Antoine's, and (d) one's departure from New Orleans, synchronicity would be achieved by scrambling the crots to present now one from group b, now one from group c, now one from group a, now one from group b, now one from group d, now one from group c, now one from group d, etc. Even if the individual crots use appropriate verb tenses (past tense primarily, with some past perfect) still the effect of the scrambling would be synchronic—all events indistinguishable within one large time frame.

Synchronicity is, of course, a stylistic effect used to support a writer's concern with the "here and now," the contemporary. Synchronicity also allows the writer to concentrate on the immediate moment and yet include matter from the past without having to compromise the discussion of the present. If, in the opinion of a writer, the only reality is what stands in front of him here and now, then his knowledge of the past is best presented in present terms. With appreciative nods toward such a history theorist as R. G. Collingwood, the writer conceives his very "knowledge of the past" as a current knowledge: knowledge *in* the present *of* the past is a synchronous situation. All in all, synchronicity provides stylistic correspondence to the "timelessness of events."

Collage/Montage. Another frequent effect of the alternate grammar of style is collage/montage in which diverse elements are patched together to make the whole composition. Easily achieved with crots and the other stylistic devices so far identified, collage/montage reacts against the "categorizing" of traditional style and insists on packaging together into a heterogeneous community all those matters that in traditional style would be grouped into homogeneous units. Quite compatible with and similar to synchronicity, the collage/montage effect (which in traditional style would be considered random, hodge-podge, patchwork) is a stylistic effort at synthesis, distinguishable from Grammar A's effort, nearly always, at analysis.

In extreme form, collage/montage can mean something as radical as William Burrough's famous cut-up method, whereby texts written in Grammar A are arbitrarily cut up, horizontally and vertically, and converted into near-unintelligible scraps of text. The scraps are then shuffled (or folded in) and joined randomly. Sometimes Burroughs carries his cut-up method so far as to cut up individual sentences into fragments, then paste the fragments back into new sentences. He does this for instance in *A Distant Hand Lifted,* wherein a typical sequence reads: ". . . remember/my/messages between remote posts of/exploded star/fold in/distant sky/example agent K9 types out a/distant hand lifted. . . ." Burroughs says this collage "method can approximate walky talky immediacy." He says further that, "Of course, when you think of it, 'The Waste Land' was the first great cutup collage, and Tristan Tzara had done a bit along the same lines. Dos Passos used the same idea in 'The Camera Eye' sequences in *U.S.A.* I felt I had been working toward the same goal; thus it was a major revelation to me when I actually saw it being done."

Less radical, and more useable, are methods of collage that use larger and more intelligible units of composition, each unit—like the crot—communicative within itself, simply being joined in the collage to other communication units, perhaps from different time periods, perhaps dealing with different subject matter, perhaps even containing different sentence/dictional style, texture, tone. Collage at its best actually countermands much of the discontinuity and fragmentation of the alternate style by revealing, by the time a composition ends, a synthesis and a wholeness that might not have been suspected at any station along the way.

As the compositional units to be "synthesized" become larger, more substantial, and more complete within themselves, we come to the sense of montage—a presentation in sequence, side by side, of compositional units less fragmental, yet fairly disparate so far as form or content is concerned. Frequently the disparate units are actually examples of various established compositional forms—e.g., poem, aphorism, letter, description, narration, anecdote, interview, questionnaire, quotation, dialogue, etc. William Blake achieved such a montage effect in the prefaces to the various chapters of *Jerusalem:* In the preface to the first chapter, for instance, he presents (a) a prose apologia for the writing of *Jerusalem,* (b) a verse apologia and address to readers, (c) a verse quatrain, (d) a brief prose theological essay, (e) a thirty-five line poem in a rough kind of iambic pentameter, (f) a three-stanza hymn-like poem made up for four-lined stanzas in generally rhymed tetrameters.

In current montage effects, writers create multi-genre compositions—using as Dylan Thomas does, for instance, in his essay "Reminiscences of Childhood," a sequence of (a) description, (b) an original poem, (c) more prose description containing (d) passages of dialogue, and ending with (e) an aphoristic-like statement, "The memories of childhood have no order, and no end."

This kind of multi-genre montage effect in the alternate style replaces, somewhat, the more traditional method of citation and quotation, though quotations themselves—in isolated forms—are often used in montage.

The use of various genres within the prose nonfiction composition—e.g., the "mimeographed schedule" in Terry Southern's "Twirling at Ole Miss"; the dramatic "scene" complete with dialogue, along with song lyrics and individual "testimonial" statements by Frank Sinatra's family in Gay Talese's "Frank Sinatra Has a Cold"; tape transcripts of earth-to-moon conversations in Norman Mailer's *Of a Fire on the Moon*—is valued by contemporary writers because it suggests that there is little difference between genres, between fiction/nonfiction in the verbal response to reality, that the category lines separating "literary forms" in the traditional areas do not really make sense if we begin to perceive reality and the verbal response to that reality in new and different ways. As Lanham says, in *Style: An Anti-Textbook*, "The fiction/nonfiction distinction is really one of differences in attitude toward prose." Hence, Norman Mailer's *The Armies of the Night*: History as a Novel, the Novel as History; and Truman Capote's nonfiction novel *In Cold Blood*.

5

Other devices/maneuvers are available in the alternate style, of course—e.g., anacoluthon, anastrophe, amphiboles of every sort—but the ones I've described are the most frequently encountered, I believe. The manipulation of these devices/maneuvers ranges from high/ornate presentations to low/plain presentations, and writers working in the alternate style have as great a range of options as do writers working within the traditional style. Obviously writers working with both styles—and their grammars—have the greatest range of all.

Compositions achieved through the alternate style will obviously be fairly open-ended in structure. That is, they will have less well-defined beginnings and endings, the composition being, to quote Baudelaire, "a work of which one could not say without injustice that it has neither head nor tail, for, on the contrary, everything in it is both head and tail, alternately and reciprocally." Compositions in the alternate style more frequently open *in medias res* and more frequently come to an abrupt stop without any well-controlled closure. The endings also have a tendency to refer back to the beginning, a la the opening and closing sentences of Joyce's *Finnegans Wake*, creating the circularity that often accompanies synchronicity and montage/collage.

Compositions in the alternate style may be of any length, of course, but there is greater tolerance for the short piece, since the alternate style is not as fallaciously committed, as traditional style is, to the "fully developed" or as frightened of the "underdeveloped." The whole composition can be, in effect, a single statement, a single observation—and can be made rather quickly. Large, full-length works—such as complete books—that are written in the alternate style have a tendency to "break down" into parts, each chapter having its own compositional quality, with some chapters even being written in traditional style, other chapters being very noticeably in the alternate style (e.g., Robert M. Pirsig's autobiographical work, *Zen and the Art of Motorcycle Maintenance: An Inquiry into Values*).

Within the alternate style, writers adhere, of course, to certain basic principles of composition: (1) A writer commits herself to one grammar of style or the other early in a composition, and once she has asked her reader to accept one style or the other, she must not "switch"; (2) Even though a writer is working within a style of discontinuity and fragmentation and even randomness, she must still be concerned with a rationale for her composition, a rationale that informs the composition, if not with "order and sense," then certainly with "interest and effectiveness"; no composition in any grammar should exist for "no reason" even if "reason" is not part of the grammar; (3) A writer in the alternate style must be especially concerned not to bore her reader, and therefore she—far more than the writer in traditional style—must be concerned with variation, variegation; (4) A writer in the alternate style must always distinguish between those devices/maneuvers that have already achieved the status of convention and those that are yet experimental; even in the alternate style, a writer needs to have agreement with her audiences about devices/maneuvers; indeed one of the main points to be made is that the devices/maneuvers we have just cited actually exist as viable conventions, with a sizeable enough audience prepared to read them and understand them.

But can the alternate style be used in *our world,* in the everyday writing class, on the college campus, for any sort of serious, academic communication? That's what we must find out. We are at the point of discovering if we as teachers of composition can now "enter the act" and bring Grammar B into the classroom, make it "legitimate" in academe. What we write, what we teach our students to write, in the alternate style will be different, of course. And the question is: is the difference worth the effort of trying new tricks, new ways of writing? What can we really produce in the alternate style?

Well, I'll volunteer to go first. And here is a "demonstration" essay that uses some of the devices/maneuvers of the alternate style and manifests (even if I've done the exercise poorly) some of its characteristics.

An Elementary Essay on William Blake's "The Tyger"

Blake's "The Tyger" (1794)/What are its sources?/ Some real tiger in the zoo?/ George Stubb's animal drawings?/ Medieval bestiaries?/ Some psychological beast within?

There are no definite answers.

Man is a zoo and within the zoo are the animals of the mind/ later in Blake there are four/ now: in *Songs of Innocence and of Experience* there are two:

Lamb	Tyger
Gentleness	Anger
Sacrifice	Authority
Receptivity	Aggression
Innocence	Experience
Child	Adult

Yet all is God: God is the mind of man: God is the full range of man's mind: God is the lamb *and* the Tyger.

So Blake asks the question: Why both things? Did he who made the lamb make thee?

Thus God makes himself: he makes himself in two parts (later in four parts) and Blake ponders the question why is it that way? Why are there such things as

Simple	Complex locutions that pre-
words	sent us with semantic puzzles
that	(riddles/enigmas) which even
everyone	though emanating from man's
can	mind defy man's mind goading
read	words into their own logomachia,
and	armies of abstractions: con-
understand	founding, obscuring, confusing . . .
	words that take arms against a
	sea. . . .

So Blake writes down the question. Showing the two contrary states of the human soul. His poem is full of the tygrrrrrrrrr.

There are no answers.

Blake draws a very gentle pussycat and paints it with stripes and puts a grin on its face. Is Blake amused?

Is God amused? Is it all a cosmic joke?

That is another question altogether/entirely. Just as no one knows where the tiger came from. One question leads to another. That's what "The Tyger" is all about: the generation of unanswerable questions: the texture of human experience.

*   *   *

Not that that exercise—or anything like it—will ever be published in *PMLA* or any other academic journal: I understand that. But I also understand that in writing the essay in Grammar B I felt a freedom to comment on Blake's poem that I would not have felt in Grammar A; in fact, I would never have attempted to say such disparate things about the poem in Grammar A. I also discovered that in "gathering my thoughts" and making my "notes," I felt—between the act of invention and the final act of composition—far less distance than I frequently have felt betwixt invention/composition while using Grammar A. (Indeed, I'm convinced that many of us in the academic world linger over our research and our studies, delaying the writing of articles and essays, because we are inwardly, unconsciously resisting having to transform our material into the forms dictated by Grammar A.) And I also realized, in writing my Grammar B essay, that while I was losing audiences on one side, I might well be making myself accessible to audiences on another. (I'm convinced that vast quantities of critical/scholarly articles and essays are ignored by many intelligent, perceptive persons who can tolerate only so many articles/essays in Grammar A in any given year.) Finally, I found a refreshing and exciting experience for myself in trying to demonstrate the devices/maneuvers of Grammar B, in discovering which ones might work for me, in discovering what I might be able to do with them.

6

Nor need our use of Grammar B in the classroom be limited to literary/ academic forms and subjects. Grammar B can actually be employed in any area of composition—even though we may find in literature the most extensive *published* instances of the style and though we may find in academic writing the greatest *need* for alternate-style fresh air.

Certainly students need not be intimidated by the alternate-style achievements of fine fiction/poetry/drama writers—when we as teachers realize, and point out to students, that Grammar B is a syndrome of style already practiced widely in personal, intimate, even very practical areas of our culture. For instance, even the mundane and pedestrian popular press, according to Eugene McNamara (in *The Interior Landscape: The Literary Criticism of Marshall McLuhan*) "affords a simultaneous model of our common existence, which we are painfully aware is scattered and broken. In a concrete immediate way, any page of a modern newspaper reflects this random disorder. The serious is juxtaposed to the frivolous, the sublime is jammed next to the ridiculous." And no doubt, the alternate style is already practiced, frequently though perhaps unwittingly, by our students themselves. (The only real nonexistence of the alternate style is in the English classroom—and that's what we're hoping to remedy.)

To help our students realize the *utility* of Grammar B (and help ourselves realize it, too) we can point out the generally unquestioned use of Grammar B in certain forms of writing (not literary, not academic) that use the alternate style extensively—personal letters, social notes, memoranda, shopping lists, diary entries, journal entries, lecture outlines—even some business letters, lab reports, resumes, grant applications, resignations, minutes of the meeting, and the like. And not only point out. We can *teach* our students the use of Grammar B in these important, quotidian forms of writing that they do and will use professionally, socially, at work, at home.

We can point out that such a simple, practical thing as a *shopping list* is usually written in Grammar B.

Butter
eggs (half doz.)
Bread
Jelly (strawberry)
2 or 3 ripe tomatoes
1 jr. coffee
2 cans chili w. beans
paper napkins
paper towels
milk, half gal. low cal
Spam
head lettuce
gr. onions
mayonaise
pizza
qt. chocolate ice crm.

It's a nice Grammar B list, of course, and I'm proud of it (I write one almost like it once a week) and I just can't imagine that Grammar A could effect a better job. How would one write the shopping list in "a more orthodox style?" Alphabetize the items? Use more perfect parallel structure? Be consistent in specifications? Neatly classify the items on the list? Not use a list at all but write out complete sentences, "I need a quart of milk. I need. . . ."?

If I were going to write the shopping list for someone else to use, I might tidy and clarify it a bit: might specify brands, sizes, quantities more adequately, might conventionalize the spelling of "mayonnaise." Yet my style would remain within the realm of Grammar B—and I can't imagine even the most rigid Grammar A practitioner thinking it necessary to restyle my list.

Or we can point out that most people write their *journals and diaries* in the alternate style.

I, for example, try to capture each day some of the moods/events/thoughts/insights that I have experienced—and though some of my "material" may benefit from a Grammar A articulation, a good deal of it would be robbed of its vitality and immediacy if I did not write it down in Grammar B. Much of my journal writing is creative—not "arty," not the creative of "creative writing class"—but the creative of immediate unhampered recollection, expression, outpouring—and that creative confrontation of the days of my life more freely comes into existence through Grammar B verbalization than through Grammar A verbalization. That's what my psyche tells me at least. And I am willing to go along with it.

Isn't that what Thomas Wolfe was doing when on Wednesday, June 22, 1938, he jotted down these impressions and experiences in his journal?

Wed. June 22.
Woke at 7:00 after sound sleep—water falling—girls voices, etc.—
Breakfast—and good one at cafeteria—after that visited waterfalls, took photographs, talked to people, visited swell hotel—sent postcards, etc., and then on way out—by the South Wawona entrance—then beautiful rockrim drive down through wooded Sierras to foothills—the brilliant leafage of scrub pine—then the bay-bright gold of wooded big barks—then the bay-gold plain and bay-gold heat—a crowded lovely road—and Clovis—lunch there—then the ride up to the mountains again—the same approach as the day before—the bay-gold big barks—then cupreous masses—then forested peaks—then marvelous and precipitous ride upward and the great view back across the vast tangle of the Sierras—then Gen. Grant and the great trees—the pretty little girls—then the 30 mile drive along the ridge

to the Sequoia—and Gen. Sherman—and the giant trees—then straight thru to other entrance then down terrifically the terrific winding road— the tortured view of the eleven ranges—the vertebrae of the Sierras — then the lowlands—and straight highroad—no bends—and Visalia— then by dark straightdown the valley—to Bakersfield—then East and desertwards across the Tehachapi range—the vertical brightness of enormous cement plants—and now at 1:30 in Mohave at desert edge— and tomorrow across the desert at 8:00 o'clock—and so to bed—and about 365 miles today.

And isn't Dag Hammarskjöld using crots and discontinuity and abbreviated sentences in this typical page from his remarkable private journal published posthumously as *Markings?*

Your responsibility is a "to—": you can never save yourself by a "not-to—".

A crack in the jug? Then you have let it get cold.

Thou who has created us free, Who seest all that happens—yet art confident of victory,
Thou who at this time art the one among us who suffereth the uttermost loneliness,

Thou—who art also in me,
May I bear Thy burden, when my hour comes,
May I—

Regard yourself as an exception, if you like: but, in that case, abandon
your hope of finding "rest in that Peace which has created the world."
(*Karin Boye*)

The body: not a thing, not "his" or "hers," not an instrument of action
or desire. In its utter nakedness—Man.

Even when journal/diary writing is destined—from the very beginning—
for publication and a literary life—its basic style remains, often enough, in
Grammar B. I think of Lawrence Durrell's *Prospero's Cell*, for instance—that
lovely well-written study of Corfu that is, essentially, a joining together of
crot-like notebook entries, devoid of any strong continuity devices.

Or we can point out that a good many *invitations* are given and accepted
in Grammar B.

The "taught" invitation is usually written in Grammar A, admittedly—
and the "etiquette book" (comparable to a Grammar A handbook) provides
us with useful patterns to follow. State occasions require stately invitations,
solemn occasions require solemn invitations, informal occasions require informal invitations. We certainly don't object to receiving—or extending—
such Grammar A invitations as the following—if the occasion, the people
involved, etc., call for them:

The President of the University requests the honor of your presence at a
luncheon the twenty-second of May in the year of our Lord. . . .

You're cordially invited to lunch on May 22 at 12:30 P.M. in the Green
Room at the Ritz Hotel. . . .

Dear Charles, I'd like you to join me for lunch on May 22 at the Ritz.
Can you meet me in the Green Room at 12:30?

We're glad to be invited. And we appreciate those variant Grammar A
styles telling us what kind of affair each lunch is going to be.

But just as valid—on other occasions, with other people—are Grammar
B invitations such as these:

Lunch tomorrow? At the Ritz? 12:30?

Agnes. 22 May. Some wine. Some quiche. Some conversation. Green Room. Ritz Hotel. 12:30. Would you like?

My treat Thursday (it's payday) at the Ritz HOT L in the "fabulously elegant" chambre verte (we'll ignore all those crummy plastic plants) where "they" *say* the seafood salad is for real and we can tete-a-tete from half past twelve until. . . .

We'd hate to be so *stuck* with Grammar A invitations (extending or receiving) that we'd miss out on (extending or receiving) these Grammar B invitations. That is, we'd hate for all our lunches to be the same—all articulated with Grammar A steadiness and air conditioning; we wouldn't mind running over to the Ritz some noon with warm Grammar B expectations. That is, we'd hate for some ersatz "teacher" to spoil our luncheon possibilities by red-penciling the Grammar B invitations ("Write in complete sentences," "Avoid slang," "Avoid foreign expressions," "Tete-a-tete is pretentious. It's also a noun. Do not use as a verb," "Avoid unnecessary repetitions," "HOT L spelling error? typo?," etc.) into well-written and proper Grammar A forms.

Or we can point out that Grammar B is used to write many a *letter*.

Yes, most business letters are written in Grammar A because in the world of business such things as clarity, economy, orderliness, reasonableness are ostensible virtues, and communications within the business world should be designed with those virtues in mind. We all agree. When I write to the oil company to complain about an error in my credit card billing, I'm eager to be clear and reasonable and orderly and economical. I'll get my bill attended to much more quickly and accurately if I proceed straightforwardly. I shall write in Grammar A—and eschew Grammar B. Unless—

Unless I find that I am corresponding with a computer. And that after the seventh letter in Grammar A I am still being threatened for nonpayment of the bill I paid two months ago. *Then* I may begin to handle my business correspondence in varying degrees of Grammar B. I may forgo that neat business-letter form—from its salutational "Gentlemen" to its complimentary "Sincerely yours" with all those complete, well-made, crystal-clear, nonredundant sentences in between. I may take advantage of a varying number of Grammar B devices to compose a letter that will get some attention from somebody! please! and that will not be so "reasonable" that it can be card-punched into the "reasonable" Grammar A program of the computer's mechanical brain. I may indeed make lists, flaunt redundancies, coin a few new words, syncopate my prose rhythm, skip transitions.

To: *Deep Well Oil Company*
From: *Credit Card: #4960-110338*

For God's sake. In February—you were wrong. March—wrong. April—wrong. May—wrong. Still wrong. It's 35$. Not 135$. Have you blown a fuse? Pleaseseepreviouscorrespondence. Five service-station tickets: $7.50 + $8.00 + $4.25 + $10.25 + $5.00 = $35.00. You must start all over again. Recompute. You must deduct $100. I've paid. Have canceled check. $35.00. Repeat. $35.00. Repeat. $35.00. I am praying for you and your circuits, but not a penny more business with Deep Well until you correct error.

A good example of the Grammar B business letter is one written by Ambrose Bierce (long before computers) to a magazine editor. Writing from The Army and Navy Club, Washington, D.C., on May 22, 1913, Bierce broke through the conventions of a Grammar A letter in order to express himself more fully—and effectively—in the alternate style:

Editor "Lantern,"
   Will I tell you what I think of your magazine? Sure I will.
   It was thirty-six pages of reading matter.
   Seventeen are given to the biography of a musician,—German, dead.
   Four to the mother of a theologian,—German, peasant-wench, dead.
   (The mag. is published in America, today.)
   Five pages about Eugene Field's ancestors. All dead.
   17 + 4 + 5 = 26.
   36 − 26 = 10.
   Two pages about Ella Wheeler Wilcox.
   Three-fourths page about a bad poet and his indifference to–German.
   Two pages of his poetry.
   2 + 3/4 + 2 = 4 3/4.
   10 − 4 3/4 = 5 1/4. Not enough to criticise.
   What your magazine needs is an editor—presumably older, preferably American, and indubitably alive. At least awake. It is your inning.
                                         Sincerely yours,
                                       Ambrose Bierce

And personal letters are nearly always written in Grammar B, whether the writer identifies his style as such or not. Rare is the pedestrian soul who "takes his pen in hand" and writes family, friends, or lovers in Grammar A. Usually in personal relationships (unless they have chilled into the impersonal or are really business relationships simply disguised as "personal"), we are willing to sacrifice some of our classroom orderliness, unity, even clarity so as to communicate our feelings, moods, realities in a more verisimilar, more emotive way. Verbosity and meanderings, intolerable in business correspondence, frequently help communicate our warmth and sincerity in personal correspondence. Vagueness and ambiguity, intolerable in business correspondence, may frequently help communicate our very humanity and uncertainties, or communicate our very "relaxedness" in personal situations. Unstructure, in personal letters, may be our very way of saying, "Look. No tricks. No masks. Just good old me."

So: real people in real personal situations write letters more like these—letters that are not radical or experimental or obscure, yet are freer and less structured than the traditional well-made letter that is used as a model in the Grammar A textbook and classroom:

March 18, 1979

Dear Folks,

Finally got here. Boat took forever from Piraeus to the island and stopped a lot of places (Kythnos, Serifos, some other islands along the way) and took about seven hours altogether, which made it almost dark on arrival.

So much to tell you. Little things. Can't get them all in this letter but will try to remember them later on in other letters.

As said, almost dark when we got here and had trouble getting a taxi but one finally came. Funny feeling. Sitting there on the dock, luggage piled around, wondering which way to go, etc. (Remember that trip we took once to Monterrey and got lost and wound up in that crazy little village? Well, it was just like that! Same weird feeling!)

Anyway, safe and sound now. Getting adjusted to Greek food, Greek language, Greek music, Greek everything. Wonderful. Want to rush this to P.O. so will stop now—but more later, of course. Just a note now so you'll know I got here and everything's O.K.

Much love,
W.

And a letter from Robert Frost to his daughter Lesley:

Amherst, 18 March 1918

Dear Lesley:

We'll all be together again soon telling funny stories.

This is the day in the week when I get a chance to do to others as still others do to you. I wonder if truth were told how many of my underlings suffer from my exactions as you suffer from poor Miss Drew's.

*Do you know I half suspect Miss Drew meant to take your sarcasm to
herself by her correction of "teacher" to "instructor". It was as much as
to say "teacher" is too general. "You aimed at me; so say instructor and
be done with it." Were you shooting at her?*

First blue bird for us this morning.

*Tell us your train of Friday and perhaps we can be at Northampton to
meet you.*

Affectionately   Papa

Enclosed is five.

And a letter written by Anne Sexton to Hollis Summers, August 31, 1959:

Dear Cousin Hollis,

*My suds, I'm back in the suburbs, the children are having an acorn
fight on the front lawn, it is 95 in the shade of the acorn tree, a ham is
cooking itself and me in the oven (my desk is situated in the dining room,
but at the door leading into the kitchen . . .)*

*All things being equal (and they surely are) I am beginning to feel and
speak like a human living woman that I am. My voice, as it descended
from Bread Loaf, had a terrifying whiskey tone (gin I guess—but the same
bloodstream voice) . . . My doctor said that I'd been on a binge. I mean,
he knew I hadn't—but I certainly attended one and did indeed partake
thereof.*

*I don't think I had a chance to say farewell to you. But I liked your
speech. I mean, I heard it. It seems important for you to know that I
listened. And besides, you know perfectly well that your yankee cousin
does not like saying goodbyes.*

*So I have been settling back since my return on Wednesday. Music,
music, music . . . my life and music music music . . . and your book OF
COURSE! . . . and have even written a poem which I will enclose for
your approval. It is only one hour old so don't be too critical. Though I
have been trying to write it, bits and starts, for six days.*

Answer me or I shall cry.

Best,
Annya

Could we, in any serious way, take a dim view of such letters because they are
not really "well made" in the Grammar A sense? Because they skip from topic
to topic, take liberties with sentence structure, flirt with non sequiturs, begin
in medias res, and the like? Can we, in any serious way, believe that the Frost
and Sexton letters, written as private letters by intelligent and educated
persons, should—on becoming "public"—be, as some Grammar A advocates
would inevitably insist, edited and "corrected"?

There are other obvious forms of ordinary communication and discourse that our students can compose using Grammar B, of course. Written interviews, yearbook features, some forms of news articles come to mind. But, without belaboring the point, we can—in essence—assure our students (and again ourselves) that

1. The alternate style is not limited to rarefied critical/scholarly writing, to experimental literature/creative writing, or to any particular kind of writing whatsoever. A writer—student, teacher, amateur, professional—decides to use Grammar B—*or* Grammar A—in consideration, not so much of the genre in which he is writing, but of the basic rhetorical situation: and the very same determinants that have always played their part in writing decisions—occasion, subject, audience, purpose, chemistry/capacities of the writer—play their part still. A knowledge of Grammar B simply gives the writer greater opportunity to satisfy those determinants.

2. The alternate style is not exclusively a private style (nor is traditional style exclusively a public style). Consideration should be given to the total range of style—in both private writing and public writing, in writing intended for oneself/a limited audience or for larger/sometimes general readerships.

3. The alternate style is not a style that "comes after" traditional style. It is not a "subsequent" skill. The old argument that you should learn traditional style first and then maybe move on to more liberated styles is invalid. Both styles are equal and essential parts of a total stylistic capacity and performance: now one, now the other: but both always a part of a total repertoire.

Indeed, if one style is anterior to the other, Grammar B has the greater claim: it is probably the fundamental and essential style, out of which a secondary Grammar A has been developed for specialized logic/clarity goals; but, because of the "system's" long inculcation of Grammar A and disapprobation of Grammar B (the sort of displacement that William Blake "howls" about throughout his prophetic work), we are led to the very need to "teach" Grammar B—a teaching that is perhaps, actually, a restoration.

7

But, dear sir, do you not realize that the stylistic maneuvers and devices that you have been describing are ultimately subversive? Surely you jest when you suggest that discontinuity and fragmentation and non sequiturs and mixed metaphors have any place whatsoever in American composition. Good writing is a discipline (in case you don't know) and discipline means order, continuity, logical development, and complete sentences! I am appalled with the whole idea of an alternate grammar of style. Yours very truly. Professor A.B.

Dear Professor A.B.: You haven't been listening. No one is suggesting that we do away with continuity, order, good paragraph development, or complete sentences. It's not a matter of elimination. It's a matter of increasing the possibilities and the options.

Dear Sir: I see no place whatsoever for such a stupid device as a "list" in serious academic writing.

Dear Madame: I admit that few academic audiences today are prepared to accept the full range of devices available in the alternate grammar of style. But the day may come.

Dear Professor W: This all sounds like creative writing to me, and I don't think we could do much with all these maneuvers and devices in a regular English class. Not at my college at least. We teach research papers and things like that.

Dear Professor K: A traditional grammar of style for some research papers, an alternate grammar of style for other research papers. Is there anything wrong with that? Why not let the research material itself help determine the style of its presentation? What is research in the first place? The acquisition of data, the investigation of evidence? Discovering, inventing, evolving new information and ideas? Compiling, evaluating, coming to conclusions? Should all that activity—creative as it often is—be inexorably marshalled toward Grammar A forms? Is it really good research if we are prejudiced in favor of one stylistic grammar—and know, even before our research begins, what the contours of our final intellectual structuring and verbalization will be?

If you think, fellow, I'm going to teach my students to write like Donald Barthelme, you're crazy.

I don't believe it's a matter of teaching anyone to *write like Barthelme or Brautigan* or *write like Joyce* or *write like D. H. Lawrence*. It's a matter of: catching sight of/ a student's catching sight of/ something in Barthelme, Joyce, Lawrence that we/a student can incorporate into composition, into more flexible communication.

Ideally, I think we should teach the alternate grammar of style alongside the traditional grammar of style, giving students the whole story of contemporary composition. I think we should simply posit, at the beginning of our instruction, the full range of styles available in both grammars, and use the two grammars tandemly, revealing the virtues of one by comparison with the other, revealing to students how nearly everything they are able to do in writing has its place in some sort of composition or other.

Even if we believe our commitment to the traditional style is so strong that we must give our full time to teaching it, we should at least acknowledge the alternate one. Say something about it. Point out its existence. Even if we exclude it from our daily work in the classroom. Even if we say to students, "We can't deal with such matters here in Freshman English" and tell them they must wait until they take advanced writing or creative writing before they can try such things, we will at least have been honest with them and not left them with the impression that traditional style is all there is. We can at least avoid, in our profession, the conspiracy of silence that is tantamount to restriction and suppression.

The important thing is that we, as teachers, know that what we usually teach in freshman English is but "part of a whole" and that we are dealing only with one area of composition. The important thing is that we, as teachers, know *about* the larger context of composition in which our particular, specialized instruction is taking place. And if our own orientations are liberal and open, I think we will perhaps open up for ourselves a whole new attitude toward the evaluation and grading and marking of the ordinary freshman papers that appear before us.

Perhaps we can stop marking *this or that* on the freshman paper as "wrong" and start identifying *this or that* as belonging to one style or another. Perhaps we can move out of a correct/incorrect syndrome into a syndrome of identification. The student writes a sentence fragment: we tell him his "fragment" is more typical of Grammar B than of Grammar A. The student mixes levels of diction: we tell him the mixing of levels of diction is more typical of Grammar B than of Grammar A. The student writes a well-developed paragraph: we tell him the paragraph is typical of Grammar A. The student writes a well-developed paragraph followed by a set of sentences that are obviously a crot: we tell him he is jumping from one style to another and probably making too great a demand on his reader; it's not wrong, but he should be very cautious.

I can mark his paper—sentence by sentence: Grammar A, Grammar B. I can help him move his paper into the grammar that is already predominant within it. Or I can help him determine the grammar that would be the more effective for his subject. And I will, of course, have to mark certain maneuvers/devices as not belonging to any established "grammar" (e.g., between you and I, its nice, the principle of our school, we went allegory hunting on the Nile). But those are matters of usage, case, spelling, and they have never been the real problems of composition. The real problems have always had to do with style and rhetoric, with "organization and arrangement" of material, with "appropriateness," with "logic." And those matters can be better understood and resolved given a knowledge of diverse grammars.

Dear Doctor: I wish to inform you that I have conducted a scientific experiment in my writing class that proves beyond the shadow of a doubt that Grammar A alone is a tenable writing style. I presented my students with ten examples of Grammar A writing and six examples of Grammar B writing; I asked my students to tell me—honestly, now, tell me—which pieces of writing they found the easiest to comprehend, the easiest to paraphrase, the easiest to explain to someone else the meaning of. I am glad to report that the students in my Grammar A writing class voted overwhelmingly—18 to 2—that they could understand and explain the Grammar A selections better than the Grammar B selections. I think you will agree that this scientific test proves that students are not at all interested in Grammar B writing; they find Grammar A writing to be more coherent, orderly, reasonable, nicer . . . and saner, I might add.

Dear Colleague: I can well understand that your students, given excellent instruction in Grammar A not only by you but by a host of previous teachers, no doubt recognize the desired Grammar A qualities in examples of— Grammar A writing. I, too, find Grammar A writing more "coherent, orderly, and reasonable." (I'm not so sure about the "nicer" and "saner.") But isn't your "scientific test" a bit like presenting a group of good ordinary people who have eaten oranges most of their working days with a pile of "oranges" and a pile of "bananas," and then asking the people, after they have tasted ten of one and six of the other, to tell you—*honestly* tell you—which pieces of fruit give the best orange taste?

Oranges will always give the best orange taste. Grammar A writing will always demonstrate Grammar A qualities better than Grammar B will. Bananas don't have a chance. Do you really want to judge bananas by their orangy quality? Is a banana somehow a worse fruit, an unacceptable fruit, because it doesn't taste like an orange? Is Grammar B beyond the pale because it doesn't do what Grammar A does?

Summary: From the experimentations with language and communication that have taken place in the last two centuries, particularly in the last hundred years, surely we can garner certain techniques, devices, maneuvers that will extend the range of composition for general and ordinary writers. Most of what we do in writing is, after all, a matter of "convention"— convention of usage, organization, structure—and surely there is the possibility that new conventions can take their place alongside the old, especially when we see before our very eyes such new conventions being practiced, not only in fiction but in journalism and other forms of nonfiction as well, by successful, widely read authors.

If we'd spend less time trying to "protect" the language from "misuse," and spend more time opening our own minds to all the things that language can do and is doing, we'd be better off.

The art of composition finally does have something to do with the art of life. Our verbal compositions become emblematic of and analogous to our social and political "compositions." If we come to composition with options, open-mindedness, adaptability, we not only fulfill ourselves the more but we obviously are capable of giving more to others.

PART TWO

Selections from Tristram Shandy *by Laurence Sterne*

In 1755, Dr. Samuel Johnson—that arch-traditionalist—was writing in the preface to his *Dictionary of the English Language* such words as these:

> When I took the first survey of my undertaking, I found our speech copious without order, and energetic without rules: wherever I turned my view, there was perplexity to be disentangled and confusion to be regulated; choice was to be made out of boundless variety, without any established principle of selection; adulterations were to be detected, without a settled test of purity; and modes of expression to be rejected or received, without the suffrages of writers of classical reputation or acknowledged authority.

Note the words "order," "rules," "purity," "classical," and "authority."

Fittingly, only five years later in 1760, Laurence Sterne began publication of his *The Life and Opinions of Tristram Shandy*—that long, delightful novel noted, as George Saintsbury puts it, for its "extremely loose and ungirt character" of style—a style "conversational, unpretentious, too easy to be jerky, and yet too broken to be sustained" that "suits subject and scheme as few others could."

Johnson with his "balanced" style—"The notice which you have been pleased to take of my labors, had it been early, had been kind; but it has been delayed till I am indifferent, and cannot enjoy it; till I am solitary, and cannot impart it; till I am known, and do not want it"—and Sterne with his exuberant "ungirt" style, set side by side, give a clear, historical demonstration of the viable coexistence of Grammar A and Grammar B even in the eighteenth century.

In the following selections from *Tristram Shandy*, we encounter radical lists, sentence fragments, tentative double-voice, vast repetitions, circularity of thought, orthographic schemes, and many other Grammar B characteristics.

*　　　　　*　　　　　*

Book Five, Chapter XV

Had this volume been a farce, which, unless every one's life and opinions are to be looked upon as a farce as well as mine, I see no reason to suppose—the last chapter, Sir, had finished the first act of it, and then this chapter must have set off thus.

Ptr..r..ing—twing—twang—prut—trut—'tis a cursed bad fiddle.—Do you know whether my fiddle's in tune or no?—trut..prut..—They should be *fifths.*——'Tis wickedly strung—tr...a.e.i.o.u.-twang.—The bridge is a mile too high, and the sound post absolutely down,—else—trut . . prut—hark! 'tis not so bad a tone.—Diddle diddle, diddle diddle, diddle diddle, dum. There is nothing in playing before good judges,—but there's a man there—no—not him with the bundle under his arm—the grave man in black.—'Sdeath! not the gentleman with the sword on.—Sir, I had rather play a *Caprichio* to *Calliope* herself, than draw my bow across my fiddle before that very man; and yet I'll stake my *Cremona* to a *Jew's* trump, which is the greatest musical odds that ever were laid, that I will this moment stop three hundred and fifty leagues out of tune upon my fiddle, without punishing one single nerve that belongs to him—Twaddle diddle, tweddle diddle,—twiddle diddle,— —twoddle diddle,—twuddle diddle,——prut trut—krish—krash—krush.— I've undone you, Sir,—but you see he's no worse,—and was *Apollo* to take his fiddle after me, he can make him no better.

Diddle diddle, diddle diddle, diddle diddle—hum—dum—drum.

—Your worships and your reverences love music—and God has made you all with good ears—and some of you play delightfully yourselves—trut-prut,—prut-trut.

O! there is—whom I could sit and hear whole days,—whose talents lie in making what he fiddles to be felt,—who inspires me with his joys and hopes, and puts the most hidden springs of my heart into motion.—If you would borrow five guineas of me, Sir,—which is generally ten guineas more than I have to spare—or you Messrs. Apothecary and Taylor, want your bills paying,—that's your time.

Book Five, Chapter XLIII

My father took a single turn across the room, then sat down, and finished the chapter.

The verbs auxiliary we are concerned in here, continued my father, are *am; was; have; had; do; did; make; made; suffer; shall; should; will; would; can; could; owe; ought; used;* or *is wont.*—And these varied with tenses, *present, past, future,* and conjugated with the verb *see,*—or with these questions added to them;—*Is it? Was it? Will it be? Would it be? May it be? Might it be?* And these again put negatively, *Is it not? Was it not? Ought it not?*—Or affirmatively,—*It is; It was; It ought to be.* Or chronologically,—*Has it been always? Lately? How long ago?*—Or hypothetically,—*If it was? If it was not? What would follow?*——If the *French* should beat the *English?* If the *Sun* go out of the *Zodiac?*

Now, by the right use and application of these, continued my father, in which a child's memory should be exercised, there is no one idea can enter his brain, how barren soever, but a magazine of conceptions and conclusions may be drawn forth from it.——Didst thou ever see a white bear? cried my father, turning his head round to *Trim,* who stood at the back of his chair:—No, an' please your honour, replied the corporal.——But thou couldst discourse about one, *Trim*, said my father, in case of need?—How is it possible, brother, quoth my uncle *Toby*, if the corporal never saw one?— 'Tis the fact I want, replied my father,—and the possibility of it is as follows.

A WHITE BEAR! Very well. Have I ever seen one? Might I ever have seen one? Am I ever to see one? Ought I ever to have seen one? Or can I ever see one?

Would I had seen a white bear! (for how can I imagine it?)

If I should see a white bear, what would I say? If I should never see a white bear, what then?

If I never have, can, must, or shall see a white bear alive; have I ever seen the skin of one? Did I ever see one painted?—described? Have I never dreamed of one?

Did my father, mother, uncle, aunt, brothers or sisters, ever see a white bear? What would they give? How would they behave? How would the white bear have behaved? Is he wild? Tame? Terrible? Rough? Smooth?

—Is the white bear worth seeing?—

—Is there no sin in it?—

Is it better than a BLACK ONE?

Book Seven, Chapter XVII

Crack, crack——crack, crack——crack, crack——so this is *Paris!* quoth I (continuing in the same mood)—and this is *Paris!*——humph!——*Paris!* cried I, repeating the name the third time——

The first, the finest, the most brilliant—

The streets however are nasty.

But it looks, I suppose, better than it smells—crack, crack——crack, crack——what a fuss thou makest!—as if it concerned the good people to be informed, that a man with pale face and clad in black, had the honour to be driven into *Paris* at nine o'clock at night, by a postilion in a tawny yellow jerkin, turned up with red calamanco—crack, crack——crack, crack— crack, crack,——I wish they whip——

——But 'tis the spirit of thy nation; so crack—crack on.

Ha!——and no one gives the wall!——but in the SCHOOL of URBANITY herself, if the walls are besh-t—how can you do otherwise?

And prithee when do they light the lamps? What?—never in the summer months!——Ho! 'tis the time of sallads.——O rare! sallad and soup—soup and sallad—sallad and soup, *encore*——

——'Tis *too much* for sinners.

Book Seven, Chapter XVIII

The *French* are certainly misunderstood:——but whether the fault is theirs, in not sufficiently explaining themselves; or speaking with that exact limitation and precision which one would expect on a point of such importance, and which, moreover, is so likely to be contested by us——or whether the fault may not be altogether on our side, in not understanding their language always so critically as to know "what they would be at"——I shall not decide; but 'tis evident to me, when they affirm, *"That they who have seen Paris, have seen everything,"* they must mean to speak of those who have seen it by day-light.

As for candle-light—I give it up——I have said before, there was no depending upon it—and I repeat it again; but not because the lights and shades are too sharp—or the tints confounded—or that there is neither beauty or keeping, &c. . . . for that's not truth—but it is an uncertain light in this respect, That in all the five hundred grand Hôtels, which they number up to you in *Paris*—and the five hundred good things, at a modest computation (for 'tis only allowing one good thing to a Hôtel), which by candle-light are best to be *seen, felt, heard,* and *understood* (which, by the bye, is a quotation from *Lilly*)——the devil a one of us out of fifty, can get our heads fairly thrust in amongst them.

This is no part of the *French* computation: 'tis simply this,

That by the last survey taken in the year one thousand seven hundred and sixteen, since which time there have been considerable argumentations, *Paris* doth contain nine hundred streets; (viz.)

In the quarter called the *City*—there are fifty-three streets.

In St. *James* of the Shambles, fifty-five streets.

In St. *Oportune,* thirty-four streets.

In the quarter of the *Louvre,* twenty-five streets.

In the *Palace Royal,* or St. *Honorius,* forty-nine streets.

In *Mont. Martyr,* forty-one streets.

In St. *Eustace,* twenty-nine streets.

In the *Halles,* twenty-seven streets.

In St. *Dennis,* fifty-five streets.

In St. *Martin,* fifty-four streets.

In St. *Paul,* or the *Mortellerie,* twenty-seven streets.

The *Greve,* thirty-eight streets.

In St. *Avoy,* or the *Verrerie,* nineteen streets.

In the *Marais,* or the *Temple,* fifty-two streets.

In St. *Antony's,* sixty-eight streets.

In the *Place Maubert,* eighty-one streets.

In St. *Bennet,* sixty streets.

In St. *Andrews de Arcs,* fifty-one streets.

In the quarter of the *Luxembourg,* sixty-two streets.

And in that of St. *Germain,* fifty-five streets, into any of which you may walk; and that when you have seen them with all that belongs to them, fairly by day-light—their gates, their bridges, their squares, their statues—and have crusaded it moreover, through all their parish-churches, by no means omitting St. *Roche* and *Sulpice*—and to crown all, have taken a walk to the four palaces, which you may see, either with or without the statues and pictures, just as you chuse—

————Then you will have seen————

————but, 'tis what no one needeth to tell you, for you will read of it yourself upon the portico of the *Louvre,* in these words, "EARTH NO SUCH FOLKS!—NO FOLKS E'ER SUCH A TOWN AS PARIS IS!—SING, DERRY, DERRY, DOWN."[1]

The *French* have a *gay* way of treating everything that is Great; and that is all can be said upon it.

Book Seven, Chapter XXV

All sins whatever, quoth the abbess, turning casuist in the distress they were under, are held by the confessor of our convent to be either mortal or venial: there is no further division. Now a venial sin being the slightest and least of all sins—being halved—by taking either only the half of it, and leaving the rest—or, by taking it all, and amicably halving it betwixt yourself and another person—in course becomes diluted into no sin at all.

Now I see no sin in saying, *bou, bou, bou, bou, bou,* a hundred times together; nor is there any turpitude in pronouncing the syllable *ger, ger, ger, ger, ger,* were it from our matins to our vespers: Therefore, my dear daughter, continued the abbess of *Andoüillets*—I will say *bou,* and thou shalt say *ger;* and then alternately, as there is no more sin in *fou* than in *bou*—Thou shalt say *fou*—and I will come in (like fa, sol, la, re, mi, ut, at our complines) with *ter.* And accordingly the abbess, giving the pitch note, set off thus:

Abbess, ⎱ Bou - - bou - - bou - -
Margarita,⎰ ————ger, - - ger, - - ger.
Margarita,⎱ Fou - - fou - - fou - -
Abbess, ⎰ ————ter, - - ter, - - ter.

The two mules acknowledged the notes by a mutual lash of their tails; but it went no further————'Twill answer by an' by, said the novice.

Abbess ⎱ Bou- bou- bou- bou- bou- bou-
Margarita,⎰ —ger, ger, ger, ger, ger, ger.

Quicker still, cried *Margarita.*

Fou, fou, fou, fou, fou, fou, fou, fou, fou.

Quicker still, cried *Margarita.*

Bou, bou, bou, bou, bou, bou, bou, bou, bou,

Quicker still—God preserve me; said the abbess—They do not understand us, cried *Margarita*—But the Devil does, said the abbess of *Andoüillets.*

---

[1] Non orbis gentem, non urbem gens habet ullam————ulla parem.

Book Seven, Chapter XXVI

What a tract of country have I run!—how many degrees nearer to the warm sun am I advanced, and how many fair and goodly cities have I seen, during the time you have been reading, and reflecting, Madam, upon this story! There's FONTAINBLEAU, and SENS, and JOIGNY, and AUXERRE, and DIJON the capital of *Burgundy*, and CHALLON, and *Mâcon* the capital of the *Mâconese*, and a score more upon the road to LYONS———and now I have run them over———I might as well talk to you of so many market towns in the moon, as tell you one word about them: it will be this chapter at the least, if not both this and the next entirely lost, do what I will———

———Why, 'tis a strange story! *Tristram.*

———Alas! Madam, had it been upon some melancholy lecture of the cross—the peace of meekness, or the contentment of resignation———I had not been incommoded: or had I thought of writing it upon the purer abstractions of the soul, and that food of wisdom and holiness and contemplation, upon which the spirit of man (when separated from the body) is to subsist for ever———You would have come with a better appetite from it———

———I wish I never had wrote it: but as I never blot anything out———let us use some honest means to get it out of our heads directly.

———Pray reach me my fool's cap———I fear you sit upon it, Madam— 'tis under the cushion———I'll put it on———

Bless me! you have had it upon your head this half hour.———There then let it stay, with a

Fa-ra diddle di
and a fa-ri diddle d
and a high-dum—dye-dum
fiddle - - - dumb - c.

And now, Madam, we may venture, I hope, a little to go on.

Selections from *William Blake*

In his essay, "The Pythagorean Genre," George Steiner (*Language and Silence*, New York: Atheneum, 1967) states that "there are other possibilities of form, other shapes of expression dimly at work. In the disorder of our affairs . . . new modes of statement, new grammars or poetics for insight, are becoming visible." He goes on to discuss writing in which he finds "the old divisions between prose and verse, between dramatic and narrative voice, between imaginary and documentary, . . . beautifully irrelevant or false. . . . Works so organized . . . that there expressive form is integral only to themselves, that they modify by the very fact of their existence, our sense of how meaning may be committed."

Then Steiner points out that "Blake would be relevant: because of his anger at set forms, because of his redisposal of statement in all manner of personal and complex spaces, part aphorism, part sung prose, part epic verse so hurtling and uncertainly stressed that the paragraphs achieve an effect of prose-poetry or *prose libre.*"

Two brief examples of Blakean writing are given here: (1) A brief tract-like essay, *All Religions Are One* (c. 1788), in which Blake emulates rational discourse (Grammar A) yet moves into the realm of Grammar B with his extreme succinctness and aphoristic quality; with his disregard of many language conventions; and with his bold use of the enumerated list as the very form of his composition. (2) *To the Public*, his "preface" to the first chapter of his final masterpiece, *Jerusalem* (1804–1820), in which he practices a kind of collage, mixing prose and poetry; edging toward language variegation with his quote from biblical Greek, his unconventional capitalizations, spellings, and punctuations; and providing a kind of vigorous apologia for Grammar B as he explains his method of poetic writing. Indeed, when he says "Poetry fettered fetters the human race," he is talking about more than poetry in the limited sense and is talking about composition in the greater sense.

✳   ✳   ✳

ALL RELIGIONS are ONE

The Voice of one crying in the Wilderness

The Argument. As the true method of knowledge is experiment the true faculty of knowing must be the faculty which experiences. This faculty I treat of.

PRINCIPLE I st That the Poetic Genius is the true Man. and that the body or outward form of Man is derived from the Poetic Genius. Likewise that the forms of all things are derived from their Genius. which by the Ancients was call'd an Angel & Spirit & Demon.

PRINCIPLE 2 ^d As all men are alike in outward form, So (and with the same infinite variety) all are alike in the Poetic Genius

PRINCIPLE 3 ^d No man can think write or speak from his heart, but he must intend truth. Thus all sects of Philosophy are from the Poetic Genius adapted to the weaknesses of every individual

PRINCIPLE 4. As none by travelling over known lands can find out the unknown. So from already acquired knowledge Man could not acquire more. therefore an universal Poetic Genius exists

PRINCIPLE 5. The Religeons of all Nations are derived from each Nation's different reception of the Poetic Genius which is every where call'd the Spirit of Prophecy.

PRINCIPLE 6 The Jewish & Christian Testaments are An original derivation from the Poetic Genius. this is necessary from the confined nature of bodily sensation

PRINCIPLE 7th As all men are alike (tho' infinitely various) So all Religions & as all similars have one source.

The true Man is the source he being the Poetic Genius

*   *   *

To the Public

After my three years slumber on the banks of the Ocean, I again display my Giant forms to the Public: My former Giants & Fairies having reciev'd the highest reward possible: the love and friendship of those with whom to be connected, is to be blessed: I cannot doubt that this more consolidated & extended Work, will be as kindly recieved

The Enthusiasm of the following Poem, the Author hopes no Reader will think presumptuousness or arrogance when he is reminded that the Ancients entrusted their love to their Writing, to the full as Enthusiastically as I have who Acknowledge mine for my Saviour and Lord, for they were wholly absorb'd in their Gods. I also hope the Reader will be with me, wholly One in Jesus our Lord, who is the God of Fire and Lord of Love to whom the Ancients look'd and saw his day afar off, with trembling & amazement.

The Spirit of Jesus is continual forgiveness of Sin: he who waits to be righteous before he enters into the Saviours kingdom, the Divine Body; will never enter there. I am perhaps the most sinful of men! I pretend not to holiness! yet I pretend to love, to see, to converse with daily, as man with man, & the more to have an interest in the Friend of Sinners. Therefore Dear Reader, forgive what you do not approve, & love me for this energetic exertion of my talent.

Reader! lover of books! lover of heaven,
And of that God from whom all books are given,
Who in mysterious Sinais awful cave
To Man the wond'rous art of writing gave,
Again he speaks in thunder and in fire!
Thunder of Thought, & flames of fierce desire:
Even from the depths of Hell his voice I hear,
Within the unfathomd caverns of my Ear.
Therefore I print; nor vain my types shall be:
Heaven, Earth & Hell, henceforth shall live in harmony

Of the Measure, in which
the following Poem is written

We who dwell on Earth can do nothing of ourselves, every thing is conducted by Spirits, no less than Digestion or Sleep. to Note the last words of Jesus, Εδοθη μοι πασα εξουσια εν ουρανω και επι γης

When this Verse was first dictated to me I consider'd a Monotonous Cadence like that used by Milton & Shakespeare & all writers of English Blank Verse, derived from the modern bondage of Rhyming; to be a necessary and indispensible part of Verse. But I soon found that in the mouth of a true Orator such monotony was not only awkward, but as much a bondage as rhyme itself. I therefore have produced a variety in every line, both of cadences & number of syllables. Every word and every letter is studied and put into its fit place: the terrific numbers are reserved for the terrific parts—the mild & gentle, for the mild & gentle parts, and the prosaic, for inferior parts: all are necessary to each other. Poetry Fetter'd, Fetters the Human Race! Nations are Destroy'd, or Flourish, in proportion as Their Poetry Painting and Music, are Destroy'd or Flourish! The Primeval State of Man, was Wisdom, Art, and Science.

"Anonymous" Valentine Letter to George Gould by Emily Dickinson

Emily Dickinson is noted for her extreme independence—both in her life-style and in her writing. In 1850, when she was nineteen years old—a good many years before she actually "retired" from the world—she wrote a valentine to George Gould, editor of *The Indicator*, an Amherst College student publication: a "valentine" in which she displayed her delight in language and her enthusiasm for keen transcendental perception of the world around her. From her earliest years, Emily Dickinson was never afraid of language; just as she developed a style of life that made sense to her and permitted her to achieve her spiritual and intellectual goals, so she developed a style of language that permitted her to give voice to observations and feelings otherwise inexpressible.

Richard B. Sewall, in his biography, *The Life of Emily Dickinson*, quotes Henry Shipley, a colleague of Gould's at Amherst, on this anonymous Grammar B valentine: "I think she must have some spell, by which she quickens the imagination, and causes the high blood 'run frolic through the veins.' " And Sewall himself finds in this "reckless and non-sequential" piece of writing, "the Orphic urge to wake up a sleeping world, to arouse her fellow mortals to the joys of living."

Emily Dickinson turned, early in her life, to an alternate style to "challenge her young friends to assault, with her, the ills of the world head-on." And in this particular example of her removal from Grammar A, we find orthographic schemes, discontinuity, strong repetitions, and other Grammar B devices incorporated into a passage of prose that explodes in freedom from orthodoxy—just as Emily Dickinson's entire psychology/intellectuality exploded free from the conventional New England patterns of her day.

Magnum bonum, "harum scarum," zounds et zounds, et war alarum, man reformam, life perfectum, mundum changum, all things flarum?

Sir, I desire an interview; meet me at sunrise, or sunset, or the new moon—the place is immaterial. In gold, or in purple, or sackcloth—I look not upon the raiment. With sword, or with pen, or with plough—the weapons are less than the wielder. In coach, or in wagon, or walking, the equipage far from the man. With soul, or spirit, or body, they are all alike to me. With host or alone, in sunshine or storm, in heaven or earth, some how or no how—I propose, sir, to see you.

And not to see merely, but a chat, sir, or a tete-a-tete, a confab, a mingling of opposite minds is what I propose to have. I feel sir that we shall agree. We will be David and Jonathan, or Damon and Pythias, or what is better than either, the United States of America. We will talk over what we have learned in our geographies, and listened to from the pulpit, the press and the Sabbath School.

This is strong language sir, but none the less true. So hurrah for North Carolina, since we are on this point.

Our friendship sir, shall endure till sun and moon shall wane no more, till stars shall set, and victims rise to grace the final sacrifice. We'll be instant, in season, out of season, minister, take care of, cherish, sooth, watch, wait, doubt, refrain, reform, elevate, instruct. All choice spirits however distant are ours, ours theirs; there is a thrill of sympathy—a circulation of mutuality—cognationem inter nos! I am Judith the heroine of the Apocrypha, and you the orator of Ephesus.

That's what they call a metaphor in our country. Don't be afraid of it, sir, it won't bite. If it was my dog Carlo now! The Dog is the noblest work of Art, sir. I may safely say the noblest—his mistress's rights he doth defend—although it bring him to his end—although to death it doth him send!

But the world is sleeping in ignorance and error, sir—and we must be crowing cocks, and singing larks, and a rising sun to awake her; or else we'll pull society up to the roots, and plant it in a different place. We'll build Alms-houses, and transcendental State prisons, and scaffolds—we will blow out the sun, and the moon, and encourage invention. Alpha shall kiss Omega—we will ride up the hill of glory—Hallelujah, all hail!

Yours, truly,

Selections from Specimen Days *by Walt Whitman*

In 1882, Walt Whitman issued his *Specimen Days & Collect*—a prose work comprising brief, self-contained passages dealing with Whitman's life, his Civil War experiences, his travels, his encounters with nature. At one point in *Specimen Days*, Whitman devotes a "crot" to the very writing itself:

> As I have look'd over the proof-sheets of the preceding pages, I have once or twice fear'd that my diary would prove, at best, but a batch of convulsively written reminiscences. Well, be it so. They are but parts of the actual distraction, heat, smoke and excitement of those times. The war itself, with the temper of society preceding it, can indeed be best described by that very word *convulsiveness*.

Whitman, in that crot, is obviously trying both to describe and to defend his Grammar B style—a description and defense he was to attempt again in 1887 when *Specimen Days* was published in England and Whitman wrote a "Preface to the Reader in the British Islands." In that Preface, he says:

> If you will only take the following pages, as you do some long and gossipy letter written for you by a relative or friend traveling through distant scenes and incidents, and jotting them down lazily and informally, but ever veraciously (with occasional diversions of critical thought about somebody or something), it might remove all formal or literary impediments at once.

Convulsiveness. Long/gossipy. Lazily/informally, Occasional diversions. Yet in what Alfred Kazin calls (Introduction to the David R. Godine edition of *Specimen Days*, 1971) this "spasmodic" book with its "slovenly, lethargic, passive ruminations," Whitman attained, Kazin says, "a seemingly directionless but actual mystical bond to the homeliest things at his feet, to street scenes, to accidental impressions and fleeting sensations . . . He was a kind of lightning conductor to things in the universe that, in the suffocatingly moral universe of so many Americans in the nineteenth century, they were to get only through him."

Everyone recognizes that Whitman in his free-verse *Leaves of Grass* achieved a grand liberation of poetic expression. Likewise, in his prose he struggled to achieve sufficient liberation from traditional style in order to say what needed to be said but had not been said before. His ellipses, his crots, his discontinuities, his lists—all contribute to a freer expression. Unintimidated by Grammar A, Whitman (to quote Kazin again), as a "wholly original writer . . . could often, despite his strange lethargies and divagations, find the idiosyncratically right word and phrase that was his essential strength—the symbol of his wholly personal way of seeing. His span of attention in these notes is short but delightful. What Whitman always did best was to make the reader partake of his homely, mysteriously effective creative process."

Through his alternate style, Whitman achieves a "communion" with his reader that is of as much value as ordinary, traditionally achieved "communication."

*   *   *

Growth—Health—Work

I develop'd (1833-4-5) into a healthy, strong youth (grew too fast, though, was nearly as big as a man at 15 or 16.) Our family at this period moved back to the country, my dear mother very ill for a long time, but recover'd. All these years I was down Long Island more or less every summer, now east, now west, sometimes months at a stretch. At 16, 17, and so on, was fond of debating societies, and had an active membership with them, off and on, in Brooklyn and one or two country towns on the island. A most omnivorous novel-reader, these and later years, devour'd everything I could get. Fond of the theatre, also, in New York, went whenever I could—sometimes witnessing fine performances.

1836-7, work'd as compositor in printing offices in New York city. Then, when little more than eighteen, and for a while afterwards, went to teaching country schools down in Queens and Suffolk counties, Long Island, and "boarded round." (This latter I consider one of my best experiences and deepest lessons in human nature behind the scenes, and in the masses.) In '39, '40, I started and publish'd a weekly paper in my native town, Huntington. Then returning to New York city and Brooklyn, work'd on as printer and writer, mostly prose, but an occasional shy at "poetry."

Typical Soldiers

Even the typical soldiers I have been personally intimate with,—it seems to me if I were to make a list of them it would be like a city directory. Some few only have I mention'd in the foregoing pages—most are dead—a few yet living. There is Reuben Farwell, of Michigan, (little 'Mitch;') Benton H. Wilson, color-bearer, 185th New York; Wm. Stansberry; Manvill Winterstein, Ohio; Bethuel Smith; Capt. Simms, of 51st New York, (kill'd at Petersburgh mine explosion,) Capt. Sam. Pooley and Lieut. Fred. McReady, same reg't. Also, same reg't., my brother, George W. Whitman—in active service all through, four years, re-enlisting twice—was promoted, step by step, (several times immediately after battles,) lieutenant, captain, major and lieut. colonel—was in the actions at Roanoke, Newbern, 2d Bull Run, Chantilly, South Mountain, Antietam, Fredericksburgh, Vicksburgh, Jackson, the

bloody conflicts of the Wilderness, and at Spottsylvania, Cold Harbor, and
afterwards around Petersburgh; at one of these latter was taken prisoner, and
pass'd four or five months in secesh military prisons, narrowly escaping with
life, from a severe fever, from starvation and half-nakedness in the winter.
(What a history that 51st New York had! Went out early—march'd, fought
everywhere—was in storms at sea, nearly wreck'd—storm'd forts—tramp'd
hither and yon in Virginia, night and day, summer of '62—afterwards Ken-
tucky and Mississippi—re-enlisted—was in all the engagements and cam-
paigns, as above.) I strengthen and comfort myself much with the certainty
that the capacity for just such regiments, (hundreds, thousands of them) is
inexhaustible in the United States, and that there isn't a county nor a
township in the republic—nor a street in any city—but could turn out, and,
on occasion, would turn out, lots of just such typical soldiers, whenever
wanted.

The Million Dead, Too, Summ'd Up

The dead in this war—there they lie, strewing the fields and woods and
valleys and battle-fields of the south—Virginia, the Peninsula—Malvern hill
and Fair Oaks—the banks of the Chickahominy—the terraces of
Fredericksburgh—Antietam bridge—the grisly ravines of Manassas—the
bloody promenade of the Wilderness—the varieties of the *strayed* dead, (the
estimate of the War department is 25,000 national soldiers kill'd in battle and
never buried at all, 5,000 drown'd—15,000 inhumed by strangers, or on the
march in haste, in hitherto unfound localities—2,000 graves cover'd by sand
and mud by Mississippi freshets, 3,000 carried away by caving-in of banks,
&c.,)—Gettysburgh, the West, Southwest—Vicksburgh—Chattanooga—
the trenches of Petersburgh—the numberless battles, camps, hospitals
everywhere—the crop reap'd by the mighty reapers, typhoid, dysentery,
inflammations—and blackest and loathesomest of all, the dead and living
burial-pits, the prison-pens of Andersonville, Salisbury, Belle-Isle, &c., (not
Dante's pictured hell and all its woes, its degradations, filthy torments, ex-
cell'd those prisons)—the dead, the dead, the dead—*our* dead—or South or
North, ours all, (all, all, all, finally dear to me)—or East or West—Atlantic
coast or Mississippi valley—somewhere they crawl'd to die, alone, in bushes,
low gullies, or on the sides of hills—(there, in secluded spots, their skeletons,
bleach'd bones, tufts of hair, buttons, fragments of clothing, are occasionally
found yet)—our young men once so handsome and so joyous, taken from
us—the son from the mother, the husband from the wife, the dear friend from
the dear friend—the clusters of camp graves, in Georgia, the Carolinas, and
in Tennessee—the single graves left in the woods or by the road-side, (hundreds, thousands, obliterated)—the corpses floated down the rivers, and
caught and lodged, (dozens, scores, floated down the upper Potomac, after the

cavalry engagements, the pursuit of Lee, following Gettysburgh)—some lie at the bottom of the sea—the general million, and the special cemeteries in almost all the States—the infinite dead—(the land entire saturated, perfumed with their impalpable ashes' exhalation in Nature's chemistry distill'd, and shall be so forever, in every future grain of wheat and ear of corn, and every flower that grows, and every breath we draw)—not only Northern dead leavening Southern soil—thousands, aye tens of thousands, of Southerners, crumble to-day in Northern earth.

And everywhere among these countless graves—everywhere in the many soldier Cemeteries of the Nation, (there are now, I believe, over seventy of them)—as at the time in the vast trenches, the depositories of slain, Northern and Southern, after the great battles—not only where the scathing trail passed those years, but radiating since in all the peaceful quarters of the land—we see, and ages yet may see, on monuments and gravestones, singly or in masses, to thousands or tens of thousands, the significant word **Unknown.**

(In some of the cemeteries nearly *all* the dead are unknown. At Salisbury, N.C., for instance, the known are only 85, while the unknown are 12,027, and 11,700 of these are buried in trenches. A national monument has been put up here, by order of Congress, to mark the spot—but what visible, material monument can ever fittingly commemorate that spot?)

The Common Earth, the Soil

The soil, too —let others pen-and-ink the sea, the air, (as I sometimes try)—but now I feel to choose the common soil for theme—naught else. The brown soil here, (just between winter-close and opening spring and vegetation)—the rain-shower at night, and the fresh smell next morning— the red worms wriggling out of the ground—the dead leaves, the incipient grass, and the latent life underneath—the effort to start something—already in shelter'd spots some little flowers—the distant emerald show of winter wheat and the rye-fields—the yet naked trees, with clear interstices, giving prospects hidden in summer—the tough fallow and the plow-team, and the stout boy whistling to his horses for encouragement—and there the dark fat earth in long slanting stripes upturn'd.

Birds and Birds and Birds

A little later—bright weather.—An unusual melodiousness, these days, (last of April and first of May) from the blackbrids; indeed all sorts of birds, darting, whistling, hopping or perch'd on trees. Never before have I seen, heard, or been in the midst of, and got so flooded and saturated with them and their performances, as this current month. Such oceans, such successions of them. Let me make a list of those I find here:

Black birds (plenty,)
Ring doves,
Owls,
Woodpeckers,
King-birds,
Crows (plenty,)
Wrens,
Kingfishers,
Quails,
Turkey-buzzards,
Hen-hawks,
Yellow birds,
Thrushes,
Reed birds,

Meadow-larks (plenty,)
Cat-birds (plenty,)
Cuckoos,
Pond snipes (plenty,)
Cheewinks,
Quawks,
Ground robins,
Ravens,
Gray snipes,
Eagles,
High-holes,
Herons,
Tits,
Woodpigeons.

Early came the

Blue birds,
Killdeer,

Meadow lark,
White-bellied swallow,

Plover,
Robin,
Woodcock,

Sandpiper,
Wilson's thrush,
Flicker.

"Hawthorne's Blithedale Romance*" by D. H. Lawrence*

By the time D. H. Lawrence published *Studies in Classic American Literature* in 1923, a number of the more startling twentieth-century demonstrations of liberated style had taken place. Gertrude Stein's *Tender Buttons* had appeared in 1914 and James Joyce's *Ulysses* had appeared in 1922. Lawrence took advantage of the writing done by the Sternes, the Blakes, the Whitmans, the Steins, the Joyces to achieve his own version of the alternate style—a style that is not really so experimental, but is rather an informed, well-crafted performance in the realm of Grammar B.

In *Studies in Classic American Literature* (from which the following "Hawthorne" essay is taken), Lawrence moved the alternate style into a prestigious forum—that of literary criticism. In the book's various chapters, Lawrence makes an intense social/cultural analysis of American literature— but not an analysis laid out in orderly one-step/two-step marshalled by a thesis. The "thesis" in any given Lawrence chapter is primarily present in the overall energetic statement weaving in and out of the text, stated this way, that way, over and around. The thesis is more "present" than "located." And in each essay of the *Studies*, Lawrence verges on a synchronicity that, if pressed only a little farther, would allow the reader to enter the text at any random point and discover on any random page the essay's "heart."

Plunging vigorously into his wrestling match with American literature/ culture, Lawrence stylistically circles and probes; lists and repeats; truncates the paragraph; plays with words; double-voices by way of the questions/ answers of an ongoing interior dialogue.

Lawrence seems intent in the *Studies* on shocking, startling, sometimes even offending. And, of course, it is only through a nonestablishment, nonorthodox style that Lawrence can escape the entrapments of decorum: in a more decorous style Lawrence would be understood—but would readers really understand the intensity of his convictions? Lawrence uses Grammar B to communicate more than thesis and demonstration; he uses alternate style to communicate his own energy, involvement—less to make us agree with him, more to provoke us into dealing ourselves with the literary/cultural issues he raises. For Lawrence, the alternate style is one of display/ stimulation—in contrast with Grammar A's proposition/proof.

*   *   *

No other book of Nathaniel Hawthorne is so deep, so dual, and so complete as *The Scarlet Letter:* this great allegory of the triumph of sin.

Sin is a queer thing. It isn't the breaking of divine commandments. It is the breaking of one's own integrity.

For instance, the sin in Hester and Arthur Dimmesdale's case was a sin because they did what they *thought* it *wrong* to do. If they had really *wanted* to be lovers, and if they had had the honest courage of their own passion, there would have been no sin, even had the desire been only momentary.

But if there had been no sin, they would have lost half the fun, or more, of the game.

It was this very doing of the thing that *they themselves* believed to be wrong, that constituted the chief charm of the act. Man invents sin, in order to enjoy the feeling of being naughty. Also, in order to shift the responsibility for his own acts. A Divine Father tells him what to do. And man is naughty and doesn't obey. And then shiveringly, ignoble man lets down his pants for a flogging.

If the Divine Father doesn't bring on the flogging, in this life, then Sinful Man shiveringly awaits his whipping in the afterlife.

Bah, the Divine Father, like so many other Crowned Heads, has abdicated his authority. Man can sin as much as he likes.

There is only one penalty: the loss of his own integrity. Man should *never* do the thing he believes to be wrong. Because if he does, he loses his own singleness, wholeness, natural honour.

If you want to do a thing, you've either got to believe, sincerely, that it's your true nature to do this thing—or else you've got to let it alone.

Believe in your own Holy Ghost. Or else, if you doubt, abstain.

A thing that you sincerely believe in cannot be wrong, because belief does not come at will. It comes only from the Holy Ghost within. Therefore a thing you truly believe in, cannot be wrong.

But there is such a thing as spurious belief. There is such a thing as *evil* belief: a belief that one *cannot do wrong.* There is also such a thing as a half-spurious belief. And this is rottenest of all. The devil lurking behind the cross.

So there you are. Between genuine belief, and spurious belief, and half-genuine belief, you're as likely as not to be in a pickle. And the half-genuine belief is much the dirtiest, and most deceptive thing in life.

Hester and Dimmesdale believed in the Divine Father, and almost gloatingly sinned against Him. The Allegory of Sin.

Pearl no longer believes in the Divine Father. She says so. She has no Divine Father. Disowns Papa both big and little.

So she can't sin against him.

What will she do, then, if she's got no god to sin against? Why, of course, she'll not be able to sin at all. She'll go her own way gaily, and do as she likes, and she'll say, afterwards, when she's made a mess: "Yes, I did it. But I acted for the best, and therefore I am blameless. It's the other person's fault. Or else it's Its fault."

She will be blameless, will Pearl, come what may.

And the world is simply a string of Pearls to-day. And America is a whole rope of these absolutely immaculate Pearls, who can't sin, let them do what they may, because they've no god to sin against. Mere men, one after another. Men with no ghost to their name.

Pearls!

Oh, the irony, the bitter, bitter irony of the name! Oh, Nathaniel, you great man! Oh, America, you Pearl, you Pearl without a blemish!

How *can* Pearl have a blemish, when there's no one but herself to judge Herself? Of course she'll be immaculate, even if, like Cleopatra, she drowns a lover a night in her dirty Nile. The Nilus Flux of her love.

Candida!

By Hawthorne's day it was already Pearl. Before swine, of course. There never yet was a Pearl that wasn't cast before swine.

It's part of her game, part of her pearldom.

Because when Circe lies with a man, *he's* a swine after it, if he wasn't one before. Not *she*. Circe is the great white impeccable Pearl.

And yet, oh, Pearl, there's a Nemesis even for you.

There's a Doom, Pearl.

Doom! What a beautiful northern word. Doom.

The doom of the Pearl.

Who will write that Allegory?

Here's what the Doom is, anyhow.

When you don't have a Divine Father to sin against; and when you don't sin against the SON; which the Pearls don't, because they all are very strong on LOVE, stronger on LOVE than on anything: then there's nothing left for you to sin against except the Holy Ghost.

Now, Pearl, come, let's drop you in the vinegar.

And it's a ticklish thing sinning against the Holy Ghost. *"It shall not be forgiven him."*

Didn't I tell you there was Doom?

It shall not be forgiven her.

The Father forgives: the SON forgives: but the Holy Ghost does *not* forgive. So take that.

The Holy Ghost doesn't forgive because the Holy Ghost is within you. The Holy Ghost *is* you: your very You. So if, in your conceit of your ego, you make a break in your own YOU, in your own integrity, how can you be forgiven? You might as well make a rip in your own bowels. You *know* if you rip your own bowels they will go rotten and *you* will go rotten. And there's an end of you, in the body.

The same if you make a breach with your own Holy Ghost. You go soul-rotten. Like the Pearls.

These dear Pearls, they do anything they like, and remain pure. Oh, purity!

But they can't stop themselves from going rotten inside. Rotten Pearls, fair outside. Their *souls* smell, because their souls are putrefying inside them.

The sin against the Holy Ghost.

And gradually, from within outwards, they rot. Some form of dementia. A thing disintegrating. A decomposing psyche. Dementia.

Quos vult perdere Deus, dementat prius.

Watch these pearls, these Pearls of modern women. Particularly American women. Battening on love. And fluttering in the first batlike throes of dementia.

You *can* have your cake and eat it. But my god, it will go rotten inside you.

Hawthorne's other books are nothing compared to *The Scarlet Letter*.

But there are good parables, and wonderful dark glimpses of early Puritan America, in *Twice Told Tales*.

The House of the Seven Gables has "atmosphere". The passing of the old order of the proud, bearded, black-browed Father: an order which is slowly ousted from life, and lingeringly haunts the old dark places. But comes a new generation to sweep out even the ghosts, with these new vacuum cleaners. No ghost could stand up against a vacuum cleaner.

The new generation is having no ghosts or cobwebs. It is setting up in the photography line, and is just going to make a sound financial thing out of it. For this purpose all old hates and old glooms, that belong to the antique order of Haughty Fathers, all these are swept up in the vacuum cleaner, and the vendetta-born young couple effect a perfect understanding under the black cloth of a camera and prosperity. *Vivat Industria!*

Oh, Nathaniel, you savage ironist! Ugh, how you'd have *hated* it if you'd had nothing but the prosperous, "dear" young couple to write about! If you'd lived to the day when America was nothing but a Main Street.

The Dark Old Fathers.

The Beloved Wishy-Washy Sons.

The Photography Business.

?   ?   ?

Hawthorne came nearest to actuality in the *Blithedale Romance*. This novel is a sort of picture of the notorious Brook Farm experiment. There the famous idealists and transcendentalists of America met to till the soil and hew the timber in the sweat of their own brows, thinking high thoughts the while, and breathing an atmosphere of communal love, and tingling in tune with the Oversoul, like so many strings of a super-celestial harp. An old twang of the Crèvecoeur instrument.

Of course they fell out like cats and dogs. Couldn't stand one another. And all the music they made was the music of their quarrelling.

You *can't* idealize hard work. Which is why America invents so many machines and contrivances of all sort: so that they need do no physical work.

And that's why the idealists left off brookfarming, and took to bookfarming.

You *can't* idealize the essential brute blood-activity, the brute blood desires, the basic, sardonic blood-knowledge.

That you *can't* idealize.

And you can't eliminate it.

So there's the end of ideal man.

Man is made up of a dual consciousness, of which the two halves are most of the time in opposition to one another—and will be so as long as time lasts.

You've got to learn to change from one consciousness to the other, turn and about. Not to try to make either absolute, or dominant. The Holy Ghost tells you the how and when.

Never did Nathaniel feel himself more spectral—of course he went brookfarming—than when he was winding the horn in the morning to summon the transcendental labourers to their tasks, or than when marching off with a hoe ideally to hoe the turnips, "Never did I feel more spectral," says Nathaniel.

Never did I feel such a fool, would have been more to the point.

Farcical fools, trying to idealize labour. You'll never succeed in idealizing hard work. Before you can dig mother earth you've got to take off your ideal jacket. The harder a man works, at brute labour, the thinner becomes his idealism, the darker his mind. And the harder a man works, at mental labour, at idealism, at transcendental occupations, the thinner becomes his blood, and the more brittle his nerves.

Oh, the brittle-nerved brookfarmers!

You've got to be able to do both: the mental work, and the brute work. But be prepared to step from one pair of shoes into another. Don't try and make it all one pair of shoes.

The attempt to idealize the blood!

Nathaniel knew he was a fool, attempting it.

He went home to his amiable spouse and his sanctum sanctorum of a study.

Nathaniel!

But the *Blithedale Romance*. It has a beautiful, wintry-evening farm-kitchen sort of opening.

Dramatis Personae:

I. *I.—The narrator:* whom we will call Nathaniel. A wisp of a sensitive, withal deep, literary young man no longer so very young.

2. *Zenobia:* a dark, proudly voluptuous clever woman with a tropical flower in her hair. Said to be sketched from Margaret Fuller, in whom Hawthorne saw some "evil nature". Nathaniel was more aware of Zenobia's voluptuousness than of her "mind".

3. *Hollingsworth:* a black-bearded blacksmith with a deep-voiced lust for saving criminals. Wants to build a great Home for these unfortunates.

4. Priscilla: a sort of White Lily, a clinging little mediumistic sempstress who has been made use of in public seances. A sort of prostitute soul.

5. Zenobia's Husband: an unpleasant decayed person with magnetic powers and teeth full of gold—or set in gold. It is he who has given public spiritualist demonstrations, with Priscilla for the medium. He is of the dark, sensual, decayed-handsome sort, and comes in unexpectedly by the back door.

Plot I.—I, Nathaniel, at once catch cold, and have to be put to bed. Am nursed with inordinate tenderness by the blacksmith, whose great hands are gentler than a woman's, etc.

The two men love one another with a love surpassing the love of women, so long as the healing-and-salvation business lasts. When Nathaniel wants to get well and have a soul of his own, he turns with hate to this black-bearded, booming salvationist, Hephaestos of the underworld. Hates him for tyrannous monomaniac.

Plot II.—Zenobia, that clever lustrous woman, is fascinated by the criminal-saving blacksmith, and would have him at any price. Meanwhile she has the subtlest current of understanding with the frail but deep Nathaniel. And she takes the White Lily half-pityingly, half contemptuously under a rich and glossy dark wing.

Plot III.—The blacksmith is after Zenobia, to get her money for his criminal asylum: of which, of course, he will be the first inmate.

Plot IV.—Nathaniel also feels his mouth watering for the dark-luscious Zenobia.

Plot V.—The White Lily, Priscilla, vaporously festering, turns out to be the famous Veiled Lady of public spiritualist shows: she whom the undesirable Husband, called the Professor, has used as a medium. Also she is Zenobia's half-sister.

Débâcle

Nobody wants Zenobia in the end. She goes off without her flower. The blacksmith marries Priscilla. Nathaniel dribblingly confesses that he, too, has loved Prissy all the while. Boo-hoo!

Conclusion

A few years after, Nathaniel meets the blacksmith in a country lane near a humble cottage, leaning totteringly on the arm of the frail but fervent Priscilla. Gone are all dreams of asylums, and the saviour of criminals can't even save himself from his own Veiled Lady.

There you have a nice little bunch of idealists, transcendentalists, brook-farmers, and distintegrated gentry. All going slightly rotten.

Two Pearls: a white Pearl and a black Pearl: the latter more expensive, lurid with money.

The white Pearl, the little medium, Priscilla, the imitation pearl, has truly some "supernormal" powers. She could drain the blacksmith of his blackness and his smith-strength.

Priscilla, the little psychic prostitute. The degenerate descendant of Ligeia. The absolutely yielding, "loving" woman, who abandons herself utterly to her lover. Or even to a gold-toothed "professor" of spiritualism.

Is it all bunkum, this spiritualism? Is it just rot, this Veiled Lady?

Not quite. Apart even from telepathy, the apparatus of human consciousness is the most wonderful message-receiver in existence. Beats a wireless station to nothing.

But Prissy under the tablecloth then. Miaow!

What happens? Prissy under the tablecloth, like a canary when you cover his cage, goes into a "sleep", a trance.

A trance, not a sleep. A trance means that all her *individual,* personal intelligence goes to sleep, like a hen with her head under her wing. But the *apparatus* of consciousness remains working. Without a soul in it.

And what can this apparatus of consciousness do, when it works? Why, surely something. A wireless apparatus goes tick-tick-tick, taking down messages. So does your human apparatus. All kinds of messages. Only the soul, or the under-consciousness, deals with these messages in the dark, in the under-conscious. Which is the natural course of events.

But what sorts of messages? All sorts. Vibrations from the stars, vibrations from unknown magnetos, vibrations from unknown people, unknown passions. The human apparatus receives them all and they are all dealt with in the under-conscious.

There are also vibrations of thought, many, many. Necessary to get the two human instruments in key.

There may even be vibrations of ghosts in the air. Ghosts being dead *wills,* mind you, not dead souls. The soul has nothing to do with these dodges.

But some unit of force may persist for a time, after the death of an individual—some associations of vibrations may linger like little clouds in the etheric atmosphere after the death of a human being, or an animal. And these little clots of vibration may transfer themselves to the conscious-apparatus of the medium. So that the dead son of a disconsolate widow may send a message to his mourning mother to tell her that he owes Bill Jackson seven dollars: or that Uncle Sam's will is in the back of the bureau: and cheer up, Mother, I'm all right.

There is never much worth in these "messages", because they are never more than fragmentary items of dead, disintegrated consciousness. And the medium has, and always will have, a hopeless job, trying to disentangle the muddle of messages.

Again, coming events *may* cast their shadow before. The oracle may receive on her conscious-apparatus material vibrations to say that the next great war will break out in 1925. And in so far as the realm of cause-and-effect is master of the living soul, in so far as events are mechanically maturing, the forecast may be true.

But the living souls of men may upset the *mechanical* march of events at any moment.

Rien de certain.

Vibrations of subtlest matter. Concatenations of vibrations and shocks! Spiritualism.

And what then? It is all just materialistic, and a good deal is, and always will be, charlatanry.

Because the real human soul, the Holy Ghost, has its own deep prescience, which will not be put into figures, but flows on dark, a stream of prescience.

And the real human soul is too proud, and too sincere in its belief in the Holy Ghost that is within, to stop to the practices of these spiritualist and other psychic tricks of material vibrations.

Because the first part of reverence is the acceptance of the fact that the Holy Ghost will never materialize: will never be anything but a ghost.

And the second part of reverence is the watchful observance of the motions, the comings and goings within us, of the Holy Ghost, and of the many gods that make up the Holy Ghost.

The Father had his day, and fell.

The Son has had his day, and fell.

It is the day of the Holy Ghost.

But when souls fall corrupt, into disintegration, they have no more day. They have sinned against the Holy Ghost.

These people in *Blithedale Romance* have sinned against the Holy Ghost, and corruption has set in.

All, perhaps, except the I, Nathaniel. He is still a sad, integral consciousness.

But not excepting Zenobia. The Black Pearl is rotting down. Fast. The cleverer she is, the faster she rots.

And they are all disintegrating, so they take to psychic tricks. It is a certain sign of the disintegration of the psyche in a man, and much more so in a woman, when she takes to spiritualism, and table-rapping, and occult messages, or witchcraft and supernatural powers of that sort. When men want to be supernatural, be sure that something has gone wrong in their natural stuff. More so, even, with a woman.

And yet the soul has its own profound subtleties of knowing. And the blood has its strange omniscience.

But this isn't impudent and materialistic, like spiritualism and magic and all that range of pretentious supernaturalism.

"The Last Parade" by E. M. Forster

No one can accuse E. M. Forster of subverting the English language. He was, as Martin Seymour-Smith calls him, a "gentle elitist," who believed, as Forster himself put it, in "an aristocracy of the sensitive, the considerate and the plucky." And in language he was a calm, sensitive stylist—who had enough good sense to use words in various interesting ways without ever violating the "good taste" that he and his kind (he was, after all, Cambridge educated and identified with the Bloomsbury group) would ever and always maintain.

In *Two Cheers for Democracy*, Forster brought together in 1951 a number of essays that he had been writing since the mid-1930s. In the opening essay, "The Last Parade" (written in 1937), and the concluding essay, "The Last of Abinger" (which is a final commonplace book entry dated Monday, July 27, 1946), Forster gives his own beautiful demonstrations of Grammar B: "The Last of Abinger" is in the manner of crots, a collection of notes; "The Last Parade" is structured in crots also—and makes vivid use of orthographic schemes, sentence fragments, etc.

Forster shows us in *Two Cheers for Democracy* the desirability for diverse grammars of style within a writer's repertoire—the validity of a writer's moving from one grammar of style to another as the nature of his/her writing tasks change. "The Last Parade" is in Grammar B, but the very last essay in *Two Cheers for Democracy*, "The Menace to Freedom," is very much a Grammar A piece as its opening paragraph tells us:

> The menace to freedom is usually conceived in terms of political or social interference—Communism, Fascism, Grundyism, bureaucratic encroachment, censorship, conscription and so forth. And it is usually personified as a tyrant who has escaped from the bottomless pit, his proper home, and is stalking the earth by some mysterious dispensation, in order to persecute God's elect, the electorate. But this is too lively a view of our present troubles, and too shallow a one. We must peer deeper if we want to understand them, deep into the abyss of our own characters. For politics are based on human nature; even a tyrant is a man, and our freedom is really menaced today because a million years ago Man was born in chains.

Definitely Grammar A. Thesis and all. And in the third essay in the collection, "Jew-Consciousness," Forster moves to a very personal style—yet still very much in Grammar A. The first paragraph reads:

> Long, long ago, while Queen Victoria reigned, I attended two preparatory schools. At the first of these, it was held to be a disgrace to have a

sister. Any little boy who possessed one was liable to get teased. The word would go around: "Oh, you men, have you seen the Picktoes' sister?" The men would then reel about with sideway motions, uttering cries of "sucks" and pretending to faint with horror, while the Picktoes, who had hitherto held their own socially in spite of their name, found themselves banished into the wilderness, where they mourned, Major with Minor, in common shame. Naturally anyone who had a sister hid her as far as possible, and forbade her to sit with him at a Prizegiving or to speak to him except in passing and in a very formal manner. Public opinion was not bitter on the point, but it was quite definite. Sisters were disgraceful. I got through it all right myself, because my conscience was clear, and though charges were brought against me from time to time they always fell through.

But when we read "The Last Parade," we read a different style, a different syndrome of stylistic behaviors. Proving: great writers can be flexible; they embrace language in its totality; they rejoice in having more styles than one to use.

In "The Last Parade," Forster uses Grammar B to confront the vast confusion of the Paris Exhibition—with its diverse salons and halls, its diverse and competing displays and sensations. Rather than attempt to organize and order his experience in a more traditional way, Forster presents us with discrete variegated blocks of vivid composition.

*   *   *

Paris Exhibition, 1937: Palace of Discovery, Astronomical Section: model of the Earth in space. Yes, here is a model of this intimate object. It is a tidy size—so large that Europe or even France should be visible on it—and it revolves at a suitable rate. It does not take twenty-four hours to go round as in fact, nor does it whizz as in poetry. It considers the convenience of the observer, as an exhibit should. Staged in a solemn alcove, against a background of lamp-super-black, it preens its contours eternally, that is to say from opening to closing time, and allows us to see our home as others would see it, were there others who could see. Its colouring, its general appearance, accord with the latest deductions. The result is surprising. For not France, not even Europe, is visible. There are great marks on the surface of the model, but they represent clouds and snows, not continents and seas. No doubt the skilled observer could detect some underlying fussiness, and infer our civilisation, but the average voyager through space would only notice our clouds and our snows; they strike the eye best. Natural boundaries, guns in action, beautiful women, pipe-lines—at a little distance they all wear the same veil. Sir Malcolm Campbell beats his own records till he sees his own back, Mr Jack Hulbert cracks still cleaner jokes, forty thousand monkeys are born in Brazil and fifty thousand Italians in Abyssinia, the Palace of the Soviets rises even higher than had been planned, Lord Baden-Powell holds a yet larger jamboree, but all these exercises and the areas where they occur remain hidden away under an external shimmer. The moon—she shows her face. Throned in an adjacent room, the moon exhibits her pockmarks nakedly. But the Earth, because she still has atmosphere and life, is a blur.

Paris Exhibition: the Spanish Pavilion, the Italian Pavilion. The other pavilions. The Palaces of Glass and of Peace. The Eiffel Tower. The last named occasionally sings. Moved by an emission of Roman Candles from its flanks, it will break of an evening into a dulcet and commanding melody. When this happens the pavilions fold their hands to listen, and are steeped for a little in shadow, so that the aniline fountains may play more brightly in the Seine. The melody swells, inciting the fireworks as they the melody, and both of them swell the crowd. O synchronisation! O splendour unequalled! Splendour ever to be surpassed? Probably never to be surpassed. The German and Russian Pavilions, the Chinese and Japanese Pavilions, the British and Italian Pavilions, any and all of the pavilions, will see to that. The Eiffel Tower sings louder, a scientific swan. Rosy chemicals stimulate her spine, she can scarcely bear the voltage, the joy, the pain. . . . The emotion goes to her tiny head, it turns crimson and vomits fiery serpents. All Paris sees them. They astonish the Panthéon and Montmartre. Even the Institut de France notices, heavy browed, dreaming of cardinals, laurels, and *réclame* in the past. O inspired giraffe! Whatever will the old thing turn into next? Listen and see. The crisis is coming. The melody rises by slight and sure graduations, *à la* César Franck, spiralling easily upward upon the celestial roundabout. Bell pop popple crack, is the crisis, bell pop popple crack, the senses reel, music and light, lusic and might, the Eiffel Tower becomes a plesiosaurus, flings out her arms in flame, the brings them back smartly to her vibrating sides, as one who should say "là!" Bell pop crack pop popple bell. The carillon dies away, the rockets fall, the senses disentangle. There is silence, there are various types of silences, and during one of them the Angel of the Laboratory speaks. "Au revoir, mes enfants," she says. "I hope you have enjoyed yourselves. We shall meet again shortly, and in different conditions." The children applaud these well-chosen words. The German Pavilion, the Russian Pavilion, confront one another again, and a small star shines out on the top of the Column of Peace.

Paris Exhibition: van Gogh. When the day breaks, van Gogh can be found if wanted. He is housed in the corner of another palace between maps of Paris and intellectual hopes for the future, and the space suffices him. Well content with his half-dozen rooms, he displays his oddness and his misery to tired feet. "Sorrow is better than joy," he writes up upon the white walls of his cell. Here are pictures of potatoes and of miners who have eaten potatoes until their faces are tuberous and dented and their skins grimed and unpeeled. They are hopeless and humble, so he loves them. He has his little say, and he understands what he is saying, and he cuts off his own ear with a knife. The gaily painted boats of Saintes Maries sail away into the Mediterranean at last, and the Alpilles rise over St. Rémy forever, but nevertheless "sorrow is better than joy," for van Gogh. What would the Eiffel Tower make of such a conclusion? Spinning in its alcove for millions of years, the earth brings a great artist to this. Is he just dotty, or is he failing to put across what is in his mind? Neither, if we may accept historical parallels. Every now and then people have preferred sorrow to joy, and asserted that wisdom and creation can only result from suffering. Half a mile off, Picasso has done a terrifying fresco in the Spanish Pavilion, a huge black and white thing called "Guernica." Bombs split bull's skull, woman's trunk, man's shins. The fresco is indignant, and so it is less disquieting than the potato-feeders of van Gogh. Picasso is grotesquely angry, and those who are angry still hope. He is not yet wise, and perhaps he is not yet a creator. Nevertheless, he too succeeds in saying something about injustice and pain. Can one look through pain and get round it? And can anything be done against money? On the subject of money, van Gogh becomes comprehensible and sound. He has got round money because he has sought suffering and renounced happiness. In the sizzle surrounding him, his voice stays uncommercial, unscientific, pure. He sees the colour "blue," observes that the colour "yellow" always occurs in it, and writes this preposterous postulate up upon the white walls. He has a home beyond comfort and common sense with the saints, and perhaps he sees God.

The Soviet Pavilion. This, bold and gleaming, hopes to solve such problems for the ordinary man. And for the ordinary woman too, who, of enormous size, leans forward on the roof beside her gigantic mate. Seen from the side, they and the building upon which they stand describe a hyperbola. They shoot into space, following their hammer and sickle, and followed by the worker's world state. The conception is satisfying, but a hyperbola is a mathematical line, not necessarily an esthetic one, and the solid and ardent pair do not group well when viewed from the banks of the bourgeois Seine. Challenging injustice, they ignore good taste, indeed they declare in their sterner moments that injustice and good taste are inseparable. Their aims are moral, their methods disciplinary. Passing beneath their sealed-up petticoats and trousers, we enter a realm which is earnest, cheerful, instructive, constructive and consistent, but which has had to blunt some of the vagrant sensibilities of mankind and is consequently not wholly alive. Statistics, maps and graphs preach a numerical triumph, but the art-stuff on the walls might as well hang on the walls of the German Pavilion opposite: the incidents and the uniforms in the pictures are different but the mentality of the artists is the same, and is as tame. Only after a little thinking does one get over one's disappointment and see the matter in perspective. For the Soviet Pavilion is a nudge to the blind. It is trying, like van Gogh, to dodge money and to wipe away the film of coins and notes which keeps forming on the human retina. One of the evils of money is that it tempts us to look at it rather than at the things that it buys. They are dimmed because of the metal and the paper through which we receive them. That is the fundamental deceitfulness of riches, which kept worrying Christ. That is the treachery of the purse, the wallet and the bank-balance, even from the capitalist point of view. They were invented as a convenience to the flesh, they have become a chain for the spirit. Surely they can be cut out, like some sorts of pain. Though deprived of them the human mind might surely still keep its delicacy unimpaired, and the human body eat, drink and make love. And that is why every bourgeois ought to reverence the Soviet Pavilion. Even if he is scared at Marxism he ought to realise that Russia has tried to put men into touch with things. She has come along with a handkerchief and wiped. And she has wiped close to the exhibition turnstiles and amid the chaos and carnage of international finance.

Park of Attractions. I did enjoy myself here, I must say. That is the difficulty of considering the Exhibition: it is in so many pieces and so is oneself. After seeing the German Pavilion, which presents Valhalla as a telephone box, and the Belgian Pavilion, which is very lovely, and many other sacred and serious objects, I sought the Park of Attractions and went up to space in a pretence-balloon. A crane lifted me into the void while another crane lowered another balloon which filled with people when my balloon was up. Then my balloon came down and the other balloon went up. So I got out and walked over the surface of the earth to the Dervish Theatre. Then I watched other people play a game called "Déshabiller vos vedettes". I thought a vedette was a boat. Here it was a tin lady, naked except for a cincture of green feathers which the entrants tried to shoot off. Then I went to a booth advertising "Perversités. Images Tourblantes." The entrance fee was a franc, which helped me to keep my head. Inside were some distorting mirrors, a little black savage who kept lashing herself or himself with a bunch of bootlaces, and some holes through which improper photographs should have been seen, but I got muddled and missed them. Oh, the French, the French! Well pleased, I came out. It was a lovely evening. The moon, which had been trying various styles from Neon to Panthéon, now imitated a pretence-balloon. The Park of Attractions, which is extremely clever and pretty, was girt with a scenic railway, and at intervals the shrieks of voyagers through space rent the night. There was plenty to spend money on. Money, money, money! The crowd was what journalists call "good-humoured"; and I, a journalist, was part of it. Tunisians and Moroccans strolled about and sometimes kissed one another. Oh, the French! Why are they so good at organizing these lighter happinesses? The English admire them, and them-selves produce the suety dreariness, the puffed pretentiousness, of Wembley.

Satan. Unexpected but unmistakable, he appears in the great entrance court of the Italian Pavilion, amongst the fragments of the lovely Italian past. These fragments are bent to his service—Garibaldi, St. Francis, Ravenna mosaics, Pompeian doves. He is to the left as one comes in, clothed all in black, and he dominates a large feeble picture of carnage. He is weakness triumphant—that is his role in the modern world. He presses a button and a bull bursts. He sprays savages with scent. He tilts his head back till his chin sticks out like a tongue and his eyeballs stare into his brain. Decent people take no notice of him or make fun of him, but presently something goes wrong with their lives; certain islands are inaccessible, a letter is unanswered, bonds confiscated, a friend takes a trip over the frontier and never returns. Elsewhere in this same pavilion are his instruments: things easily let off. He has only one remark to make: "I, I, I". He uses the symbols of the sacred and solemn past, but they only mean "I". Here, among superficial splendours of marble, he holds his court, and no one can withstand him except van Gogh, and van Gogh has nothing to lose. The rest of us are vulnerable, science is doing us in, the Angel of the Laboratory switches off the fireworks, and burns up the crowd without flame.

Meanwhile, and all the while, the Earth revolves in her alcove, veiled in wool. She has sent samples of her hopes and lusts to Paris; that they will again be collected there, or anywhere, is unlikely, but she herself will look much the same as soon as one stands a little back in space. Even if the Mediterra-nean empties into the Sahara it will not make much difference. It is our clouds and our snows that show.

Five Letters to the Ford Motor Company
by Marianne Moore

In 1955, Marianne Moore—noted American poet—was invited by the Ford Motor Company to contribute names that might be considered by the company for their new automobile model. Though none of Miss Moore's suggestions were used, her participation in the "name hunt" became famous because it betokened the kind of cooperation between industry and the arts that many intelligent people applaud. The Ford Motor Company finally selected the name "Edsel" for their new car—but Miss Moore's letters (five of which are printed here) identify fascinating other possibilities. And more to our purpose: her letters suggest a way of corresponding with a giant corporation that escapes the limiting models of formal business writing. Certainly, Miss Moore's Grammar B letters (with lists, orthographic schemes, *in medias res* beginnings, etc.) show that the alternate style, without seriously interfering with communication, can—at least on some occasions—contribute a joyous and witty dimension to ordinary business forms.

November 13, 1955

Dear Mr. Wallace:

The sketches. They are indeed exciting; they have quality, and the toucan tones lend tremendous allure—confirmed by the wheels. Half the magic—sustaining effects of this kind. Looked at upside down, furthermore, there is a sense of fish buoyancy. Immediately your word "impeccable" sprang to mind. Might it be a possibility? The Impeccable. In any case, the baguette lapidary glamour you have achieved certainly spurs the imagination. Car-innovation is like launching a ship—"drama."

I am by no means sure that I can help you to the right thing, but performance with elegance casts a spell. Let me do some thinking in the direction of impeccable, symmechromatic, thunderblender. . . . (The exotics, if I can shape them a little.) Dearborn might come into one.

If the sketches should be returned at once, let me know. Otherwise, let me dwell on them for a time. I am, may I say, a trusty confidante.

I thank you for realizing that under contract esprit could not flower. You owe me nothing, specific or moral.

Sincerely,
Marianne Moore

November 19, 1955

Some other suggestions, Mr. Wallace, for the phenomenon:

THE RESILIENT BULLET
or Intelligent Bullet
or Bullet Cloisonné or Bullet Lavolta

(I have always had a fancy for THE INTELLIGENT WHALE—*the little first Navy submarine, shaped like a sweet potato; on view in our Brooklyn Yard.)*

THE FORD FABERGE

(That there is also a perfume Fabergé seems to me to do no harm, for here allusion is the original silversmith.)

THE ARC-en-CIEL *(the rainbow)* ARCENCIEL?

Please do not feel that memoranda from me need acknowledgment. I am not working day and night for you; I feel that etymological hits are partially accidental.

The bullet idea has possibilities, it seems to me, in connection with Mercury (with Hermes and Hermes Trismegistus) and magic (white magic).

Sincerely,
Marianne Moore

November 28, 1955

Dear Mr. Wallace:

MONGOOSE CIVIQUE

ANTICIPATOR

REGNA RACER *(couronne à couronne) sovereign to sovereign*

AEROTERRE

Fée Rapide (Aérofée, Aéro Faire, Fée Aiglette, Magi-faire) Comme Il Faire

Tonnere Alifère (winged thunder)

Aliforme Alifère (wing-slender, a-wing)

TURBOTORC *(used as an adjective by Plymouth)*

THUNDERBIRD *Allié (Cousin Thunderbird)*

THUNDER CRESTER

DEARBORN *Diamante*

MAGIGRAVURE

PASTELOGRAM

I shall be returning the sketches very soon.

M.M.

December 6, 1955

Dear Mr. *Wallace:*
  Regina-rex
  Taper Racer   Taper Acer
  Varsity Stroke
  Angelastro
  Astranaut
  Chaparral
  Tir à l'arc (bull's eye)
  Cresta Lark
  Triskelion (three legs running)
  Pluma Piluma (hairfine, feather-foot)
  Andante con Moto (description of a good motor?)
  My *findings thin, so I terminate them and am returning the sketches.*
Two *principles I have not been able to capture: 1, the topknot of the*
peacock *and topnotcher of speed. 2, the swivel-axis (emphasized*
elsewhere), *like the Captain's bed on the whaleship, Charles Morgan—*
balanced *so that it levelled whatever the slant of the ship.*
  If *I stumble on a hit, you shall have it. Anything so far has been*
pastime. *Do not ponder appreciation, Mr. Wallace. That was embodied*
in *the sketches.*

M.M.

  I *cannot resist the temptation to disobey my brother and submit*
  TURCOTINGA *(turquoise cotinga—the cotinga being a South-American*
finch *or sparrow) solid indigo.*
  (I have a three-volume treatise on flowers that might produce something
but *the impression given should certainly be unlabored.)*

December 8, 1955

Mr. *Wallace:*
  May *I submit* UTOPIAN TURTLE-TOP? *Do not trouble to answer unless*
you *like it.*

Marianne Moore

"The Death of James Dean" by John Dos Passos

Though John Dos Passos is most noted for his fiction, he demonstrates in this retrospective profile of James Dean (published in 1958 in the 25th-anniversary issue of *Esquire*) the use of alternate style in the realm of popular magazine journalism. Dos Passos wrote his biographical sketch—of a rebel-without-a-cause movie star who died young—in a style that says something not only about the person but the times, not only about the actor but the Hollywood industry itself.

Dos Passos shows us that style can be used both to help emulate subject matter and to force readers into new considerations of subjects and ideas. Just as Grammar A can both imitate/be appropriate to a reasonable subject and at the same time encourage readers intellectually to negotiate even unreasonable subjects in a reasonable manner, so—Grammar B can help recreate the unstructured/less-than-logical topic and at the same time provoke readers into considering the discontinuous, nonsequential, unconventional underside of what superficially may be smooth as a syllogism and as "proper" as high tea.

J. Mitchell Morse, in *Matters of Style*, suggests that Dos Passos's famous Grammar B device of montage/collage (as developed by cubist painters) is "the juxtaposition of disparate elements in order to convey the sense of a scene—or a culture—made up of disparate elements."

Disparate elements of life: Grammar B. The erratic, unfulfilled life of James Dean: Grammar B. Portrait/biography that could have been presented in Grammar A—presented creatively, effectively in Grammar B. Portrait/profile/biography involving more than fact, involving commentary, opinion, emotional attitude—more thoroughly, freely expressed, in this case at least, in the alternate grammar of style.

*   *   *

BRONX YOUTH 16 SEIZED
IN TEEN-AGE GANG KILLING
Woman Fights for Life with Child's Kidney

Royally beautiful former Queen Soraya of Iran arrived in Genoa tonight en route to the United States saying she feels "that life starts anew for me today." Soraya talked between bites from a salami sandwich, which she washed down with synthetic orange juice from a bottle.

TEEN-AGE DANCES SEEN THREATENED
BY PARENTS' FAILURE TO COOPERATE
MOST OFFENDERS EMULATE ADULTS

James Dean is three years dead but the sinister adolescent still holds the headlines.

James Dean is three years dead;

but when they file out of the close darkness and the breathed-out air of the second-run motion-picture theatres where they've been seeing James Dean's old films

they still line up:

the boys in the jackboots and the leather jackets, the boys in the skin-tight jeans, the boys in broad motorbike belts,

before the mirrors in the restroom

to look at themselves

and see

James Dean;

the resentful hair,

the deep eyes floating in lonesomeness,

the bitter beat look,

the scorn on the lip.

Their pocket combs are out; they tousle up their hair and pat it down just so;

make big eyes at their eyes in the mirror

pout their lips in a sneer,

the lost cats in love with themselves,

just like James Dean.

The girls flock out dizzy with wanting

to run their fingers through his hair, to feel that thwarted maleness; girl-boy almost, but he needs a shave. . . . "Just him and me in the back seat of a car. . . ." Their fathers snort,

but sometimes they remember: "Nobody understood me either. I might have amounted to something if the folks had understood."

The older women struggle from their seats wet-eyed with wanting

to cuddle, to mother (it's lack of mother love makes delinquents), to smother with little attentions the poor orphan youngster,

the motherless, brotherless, sisterless, lone-wolf brat strayed from the pack,

the poor mixed-up kid.

LACK OF PARENTAL LOVE
IS BLAMED IN SLAYING

Niagara Falls, N.Y. (AP): Judge Frank J. Kronenberg says the slaying of Johnny Stompanato by Lana Turner's daughter is a *"perfect* example" of the juvenile-delinquency situation in this country. "I think the facts in this case cry out for the American public to be more discriminating in the purchase of a movie ticket."

LANA BARES HEARTBREAK
IN LOVE LETTERS TO PAPITO

From her lofty pinnacle as reigning movie queen and one of the world's most envied women, Lana Turner, rich and beautiful, reached down into the back alleys of Hollywood to surrender her heart to the strange and mysterious John Stompanato.

The press agents told us James Dean lacked parental love, that he was an orphan, a farm boy who couldn't get along at school, a poor mixed-up kid from the black-soil belt in Indiana. (He never could quite get rid of that Hoosier twang . . .

. . . Hoosier ghosts of forgotton Penrods, crackerbarrel reveries. . . . *"The thoughts of youth are long, long thoughts"* . . . *"For I was once a barefoot boy"* . . . *Life on the Mississippi. The Arkansas Traveller.* Hundred-year-old Huck Finn drifing with runaway Jim downriver on their eternal raft.) The young used to be comical in America. Not often anymore.

TEEN-AGERS TERRORIZE CALIFORNIA TOWN

Hollister, Calif.: A swarm of motorcyclists descended today on this quiet California town, breaking windows, tearing down signs, wrecking bars in an orgy of vandalism that drove the inhabitants to take refuge in their homes.

"I'm a serious-minded and intense little devil," the movie magazines quoted James Dean as saying, "terribly gauche and so tense I don't see how people stay in the same room with me. I know I wouldn't tolerate myself."

The teen-agers approve: "Everything he said was cool."

In mid-century America the barefoot boys are all shod in loafers.

The Hoosier farm boys have no cows to milk before day, no wood to chop, no horses to currycomb or oats to measure out into the manger, no coal-oil lamps to fill, no chores—"If it's housework let mother do it"—no chapter of the Bible to read every night,

no roaring preachers to remind them from the pulpit every Sunday that good is Heaven and bad is Hell,

no examiners to ask hard questions;

only perhaps an occasional package to carry out from the A & P, or maybe the family car to wash

before driving down to the drugstore for a Coke and a cigarette of some advertised brand, and a comic book (nothing in mid-century America is less comical than a comic) diagraming murder and mayhem and rape, tirelessly strumming on the

raw nerves

for kicks.

8 INDICTED IN SALE OF SMUT RECORDS

Daytona Beach, Fla., Feb. 26: National Guard troops with loaded carbines moved in early today to help break up a riot of teen-agers. The mob had flouted police authority and milled through a business section near the ocean beach for more than four hours. The riot stemmed from efforts of the police to stop a group of youths from racing their cars on ramps leading to the beach and from signal lights on the city streets. Instead of dispersing, the youths slashed the tires of two police cars and started throwing rocks. They seemed to have an idea a teen-ager had been arrested and kept calling: "Bring him back. Bring him back."

Kicks are big business: the sallow hucksters needle the nerves. Through radios drumming rock 'n roll and blurred girls crooning on TV
they hammer on the wracked nerves:
buy,
buy speed, buy horsepower, buy chromium, buy happiness in a split-level ranch house, elegance in shocking-pink lipstick, passion in a jar of Parisian perfume,
or that portable transistor set
you can take along on your vacations
so that even beside the thunderous ocean, or camping out in some hidden intervale green in a notch of the hills, you'll never be free
from the clamor of salesmen.

Why not resentful? There's more to life; the kids know it. Their fathers won a war, but weren't men enough to keep the peace; they let the pundits and the politicians wheedle them into defeat; they let the goons pilfer their pay checks, too busy watching TV to resent oppression. . . . (Freedom, What good is it? Let's have social security
and welfare and tailfins on our cars
and packaging)
. . . There's no cellophane can protect the glory of life when you've lost it; the kids know it

"When we spotted 'Killer' on the stoop of his home, he kicked Candelaria in the leg and ran for the roof. We took after him. When we reached the top landing 'Killer' leaned down from the roof and let go with his shotgun twice."

Why not resentful? Even in success James Dean was resentful. This kid had talent. That's how he differed from the general run of drugstore cowboys. The critics said he had the makings of a great film actor. He won awards. Even after he was dead the audiences voted him the best actor of the year.
"Rare mixture of truth, beauty and fun."
James Dean was resentful, we were told,
because he came from a broken home. "My mother died on me when I was nine years old. What does she expect me to do? Do it all myself." His

father married again. An aunt and uncle raised him on their neat farm in Fairmount, Indiana. He was a moody boy. He was terribly nearsighted. He did poorly in his studies,

but in high school he played baseball, basketball, led the track team and excelled in dramatics. They gave him a medal for the best all-around athlete, senior year.

His elocution teacher took a fancy to him. She spotted the talent. She coached him in parts in school plays and had him win a statewide contest in public speaking

reading *The Madman,* by Dickens.

When she induced him to enter a national contest held out in Colorado, the judges passed him over. He resented that. He never forgave that poor teacher.

His father worked as a dental technician in Los Angeles. After young Dean graduated he went out to stay with his father. There he met a fellow who was taking a course in acting with a retired motion-picture performer. James Dean tagged along; he panicked the class acting the part of a pine tree in a storm. Now he knew he wanted to act.

CITY TO ADD POLICE AT SUMMER SPOTS

He hung around L.A., broke most of the time, working as an usher in movie theatres, getting an occasional part as an extra on the lots, or a bit on TV,

dreaming and yearning and hungry,

eating cold spaghetti out of a can.

Dirty shirt, never a haircut, needed a shave, the grubbiest guy in town. Sometimes he got a job parking cars in a parking lot to earn the two bits he needed for a hamburger and a cup of coffee.

HOUSEWIFE'S DOLLAR
SHRINKS SOME MORE

RESERVE BANK'S HEADS SAY
CONSUMER'S RECOVERY IS KEY

The three juvenile gangs involved in the arrest yesterday of a 20-year-old boy on charges of killing a rival gang member have a characteristic in common. They are the "shook-up generation" in sections of the city undergoing their own profound shake-ups in social patterns.

James Dean was impatient. He was stagnating in L.A. He made a break for New York, rode east all the way on the bus. For a year he hung around Broadway with out-of-work actors.

ONE WORKER IN FOUR FOUND
DEPENDENT ON FOREIGN TRADE

As he mounted the steps a photographer said, "Look up."

"You are not the Sinners," the youth replied. "I don't have to look up to you." Inside the station, however, the prisoner told the police: "I'm sorry I shot him. I didn't mean to pull the trigger. I only meant to cock the gun."

"New York is vital, above all, fertile," James Dean used to tell the reporters. "I fit into cadence and pace better here."

He developed a lingo
out of tearoom talk about be-bop and Bach,
and stale shards of Freud,
existentialism,
and scraps out of translations of Jean Genêt sold under the counter:
—"Our Lady of the Flowers"—
include me out: self-expression.

In the drab summer desert of New York, James Dean lacked friends; he lacked girls, he lacked dough;

but when the chance comes he knows how to grab it; a young director takes an interest, invites him out sailing on a sloop on the Sound, gives him a part in a show which immediately flops;

but he's been seen on the stage. He plays the blackmailing Arab in a dramatization of André Gide's *Immoralist.* He walks out on the part, the play closes, but he's been seen by people who know show business: rave write-ups: he's an actor.

Live the part, Stanislavsky told his actors.

Dean does just that. He's obstreperous as hell. "I can't divert into being a social human being," he snarls at the reporters through the butt that dangles from his lip, "when I'm working on a hero like Cal who's essentially demonic."

The tall muscular youth was arrested as the result of a trap set for him by the police. They had the cooperation of his girl friend who was among the fifty youngsters questioned by the police yesterday morning. Two detectives accompanied the girl to their usual meeting place. They hid in two hallways. The other detectives also kept out of sight. When Serra walked to the girl the detectives surrounded him.

He was wearing a narrow-striped red-and-grey blazer. A tiny gold cross was attached to the lobe of his left ear.

Demonic, but lovable under it all.

The sinister adolescent is box office. Long before his first picture is released James Dean is besieged by Hollywood agents, promoters, feature writers, photographers.

He is serious about self-expression. "Acting is the most logical way for people's neuroses to express themselves." As soon as he's in the money he buys himself a good camera and photographs himself in melancholy moods,
     sad and resentful and sorry, so soon to die,
     but lovable under it all. Sharp lights and shadows, his head in a noose, a kitchen knife shot for a dagger. He talks a lot about wanting to sculpt.
     He's crazy about racing cars. Speed's how to die. He makes up his own mobiles. He's planning to be a bullfighter: "Death in the Afternoon."
     "Cool," echo the teen-agers. "Everything he said was cool."
     In Hollywood he goes on playing the part he plays on the screen. "A wary suspicious loner," one director calls him. Another is more forgiving: "Just a boy on the rise."
     "Rebel Without a Cause."
     The teen-agers saw themselves in James Dean. Everything he said was cool.

Screening *Giant*,
     he was already beginning not to like it much if people didn't look up when he slouched into the Villa Capri that was his hangout. Wasn't he James Dean?
     He was handy with the mambo drum. His bachelor actor's home was loud with hi-fi. He had to pick an isolated location so that the neighbors wouldn't complain about the rock 'n roll. . . .

7 TEEN KILLERS IN JURY'S
HANDS AFTER NINETY-FIVE DAYS

The king of the disc jockeys was throwing a ball so I decided to ankle along. There must have been a thousand more cats than they had seats for. They started off with cool numbers, but pretty soon they speeded up. As the music got warmer so did the cats. They started climbing out of their seats, running up and down the aisles screaming to their buddies. One kid dressed in a leather jacket and paratroop boots stood up in his seat and started to wave his arms. Four cops tried to take him out. Before long, twenty or thirty kids had pitched in to help him and everybody else was yelling like crazy and tossing things at the cops.
     James Dean is made. In quiet moods he likes to be seen in Hollywood night spots with another celebrity. He plays around with the girl who acts Vampira on TV, the ghoul who gives people, right in their own homes, their daily creeps,
     like a Charles Addams cartoon. (No romance, say their friends, and how she was real warmhearted underneath and understood his resentments.) He tells her everything.
     A few days before his death she sends him a postcard picture of herself posed beside an open grave. "Come join me," it reads.

TWO THEORIES OFFERED
AS CLUES TO ALL MATTER

Dean owned a horse, but racing cars was his public hobby. He'd won a race for novices at some meet. His racing had given the producers fits. He teased them by telling them that racing was a glorious way to die. (Life can't be all Social Security and safety first. The kids know that. It's glory a man has to have.) Some friends furnished him with a St. Christopher medal, but the studio had written it into his contract that he wasn't to race a car until the picture was ready for release.

By September 30, 1955, he was free from that clause in his contract. There was to be a meet at Salinas. Instead of taking his white Porsche Spyder with the 130 painted on its side over to the track on a truck like most of the contestants,

he had to drive it over himself. His German mechanic went along. A photographer followed in a station wagon.

He wanted to feel her speed.

Already at Bakersfield a traffic cop gave him a ticket for doing sixty through a forty-mile zone.

The sun was setting. It was nearly dusk. He wanted to feel her speed. He was making seventy-five, eighty, a hundred—accounts differ—when near Paso Robles on the empty highway he collided head on with a car turning in from an intersection,

a Ford driven by a young man named Donald Turnupseed.

James Dean was killed. The steering wheel went through him: Turnupseed and the mechanic were hurt but recovered.

Fairmount, Indiana, October 8: James Dean, the motion-picture actor, was buried today in a quiet country ceremony in the community where only six years ago he had been an outstanding high-school athlete. A crowd estimated at 3000 milled quietly about this little town of 2600 people as final services were read.

Dead at twenty-four:

"James Dean can't be dead," the girls told each other, "he's in the hospital undergoing facial surgery." It would take a long time, but someday they would see him slouching out onto the screen again.

People paid fifty cents a head to see the wreck of his car.

In L.A. the clairvoyants and psychics did a land-office business interviewing James Dean in the spirit world. Some interviews were printed. "Everything he said was cool," the teen-agers said.

At Warner Brothers the requests for photographs, which had merely been average, went up by the time he'd been dead a year to seven thousand letters a month. Everybody from his grandmother to the waiters at the Villa Capri was interviewed by the motion-picture press. The pulp merchants sold one-shot lives of him in hundreds of thousands of copies. Bronze heads and plaster masks were marketed in bulk.

One popular item was made of a plastic supposed to feel like human skin when you stroked it.

Candelaria was found moaning on the fifth-floor landing of the Fox Street tenement. Mrs. Retorico, a registered nurse, almost fainted when she heard her son named as the gunman, but she said nothing and concentrated on giving the victim first aid. "He could hardly whisper," Chavez said, "his clothes and body were torn to shreds. But he recognized that we were trying to help him. 'Help me, I'm going to die.' "

"The Killer" was taken to the Simpson Street Station for booking. He glowered behind dark glasses.

The sinister adolescents come to various ends.

They found it hard to believe that James Dean was dead. There he was right on the screen when they saw his old pictures. The promoters had been struggling hard to blow up the story that millions wouldn't believe he was dead, but when they released a picture on his life nobody went to see it. When a man's dead, he's dead. His competitor, Elvis Presley, continued the rage, bumping his guitar with his rump,

until his draft board one day
drafted him into the Army.

U.S. CAN HIT MOON IN '58
OFFICER SAYS

The sinister adolescents come to various ends; sometimes they grow up.

"Facing Facts" by Susan Lardner

In this *New Yorker* (June 20, 1977) book review, Susan Lardner makes excellent use of the alternate style to criticize Joan Didion's *A Book of Common Prayer*. Admittedly, Lardner's Grammar B is achieved by parodying the "style" of Didion's novel, but the style in this review is more than just a "making fun" of Didion's manner: it is commentary and criticism in the serious sense, written in the alternate style because the traditional style would have demanded a more orderly, organized handling of the Didion novel that would have betrayed Lardner's critical evaluation.

In her book review, Lardner is not only *telling* us about Didion's novel— but is also *showing* us something about it. And the very fact that Lardner is taking a critical stance contrary to the opinion of others—(Didion has "firmly established her position as a major American writer" and has "written her strongest and most powerful book to date")—she uses Grammar B, not only as parody, but also as protest. Moving out of the realm of "given opinion," she moves out of traditional book review style to present her dissent.

In her use of clipped sentences, non sequiturs, illogical leaps, lists, non-paragraphs, etc., Lardner gives a convincing performance: the alternate style can be used in yet another form of popular journalism and can effectively reach a large sophisticated audience.

✳   ✳   ✳

I will testify.

That is to say, I have read Joan Didion's latest book and would tell you in my own words what it is like were it not that I have been alienated from my own words by a syntax so compelling that I cannot now be sure what it was that I did or did not think of the book or of anything at all before I was struck by this feeling of cerebral dysaesthesia.

Let me go further.

I have no idea what I mean by "cerebral dysaesthesia."

Here is what I know: Didion wrote one novel, "Run River"; she wrote articles for magazines, and these may be found collected under the title "Slouching Towards Bethlehem"; she wrote a second novel, "Play It As It Lays," and I am without doubt that there she achieved a nearly perfect match of style and character.

You may know the book.

You may remember its heroine—as it happens, an actress the author called Maria Wyeth.

Maria was losing her grip on reality and her marriage was going to pieces and she had a four-year-old daughter institutionalized because of "an aberrant chemical in her brain," and then there was the abortion and the lovers who left her cold.

In short.

But Maria was tough. She knew that life is a crap game and that actually there is a rattlesnake under every rock. She never asked silly questions like "What makes Iago evil?" She knew there were no answers.

She knew what "nothing" meant.

Or so she said.

Why go on living?

On the contrary, why not?

So.

Maria went on living.

Didion has, of course, gone on writing.

Has, in fact, "firmly established her position as a major American writer." Has in her third novel "written her strongest and most powerful book to date." I offer here only empirical evidence and jacket copy.

(Had I not set out to stick to the facts, I would have said that in her third novel Didion has converted a perfunctory rhetorical habit into a positive affectation of style.)

One or two facts about the third novel Didion wrote and I read: It is published by Simon & Schuster: "A Book of Common Prayer" is its title, and the title signifies the principal irony of the plot, although to a reader immaculate of the author's equivocal disenchantment "prayer" would at first seem to be beside the point.

As though two such disparate characters as Grace Strasser-Mendana and Charlotte Douglas might not have cause for a joint appeal against shared disappointments.

But, of course, they do.

For one thing: thinking it over, I recalled that Grace had admitted as much in a remark about Charlotte's dreams—had said that "these dreams seemed to deal only with sexual surrender and infant death, commonplaces of the female obsessional life."

"We all have the same dreams," Grace had added.

Grace the "realist," dying of cancer.

Grace the narrator, learned in science and in the human weakness for self-deception. She never asks silly questions like "What makes me talk the way I do? What makes me say things like 'Fear of the dark is a protein'?

"Like 'What I wanted from the interior had nothing to do with access.'

"Like 'There is poverty here, but it is obdurately indistinguishable from comfort.'

"Like 'I think I have never known anyone who regarded the sexual connection as quite so unamusing a contract.'

"Like 'In a certain dim way Charlotte believed that she had located herself at the very cervix of the world, the place through which a child lost to history must eventually pass.' "

I believe I would say that last one is my favorite.

The setting, by the way, is an invented Central American country called Boca Grande. Notable for its disobliging equatoriality.

I am less and less certain that the word "equatoriality" has any useful meaning except insofar as it denotes a non-polar location.

As for Charlotte, Charlotte is a sentimental woman, a "dreamer," the subject of the story told by Grace.

Charlotte yearns for her lost daughter, refuses to admit that the child has abandoned Raggedy Ann and organdie curtains for a life of pipe bombs, plane hijacking, and "revolutionary" broadcasts.

Herself killed in a revolution. Charlotte.

A dead dreamer.

Still. She killed a chicken bare-handed and tracheotomized an O.A.S. man with a boning knife.

For the record. "A Book of Common Prayer" contains references to the following pathological conditions: influenza, pancreatic cancer, infant framboesia, schistosomiasis, cholera, gastrointestinal infection, *la disenteria*, typhoid, salmonella, convulsions, projectile vomiting, nausea, neurasthenia, and tuberculosis.

Among others.

In summary: Life is hell.

Had Grace only been able to make Charlotte see her point. When she told her that fear of the dark was a protein.

Had Charlotte only been less ambiguous in her signals, less elusive in her anomalies, and enabled Grace, or for that matter, the reader, to see *her* point.

But, of course, they don't.

See each other's points.

For the record. It would not have mattered.

Apparently.

Probably.

Still.

So.

"Other Obstacles, Balks, Encumbrances in Coming to One's Own Voice, Vision, Circumference" by Tillie Olsen

Tillie Olsen—author of the classic *Tell Me a Riddle*—deals with all sorts of "encumbrances" that prevent writers/would-be writers/student-writers/teachers-of-writing from getting said what they have within themselves to say. Especially concerned in *Silences* (New York: Delacorte, 1978)—from which the following essay is taken—with the various forces/situations that keep women "shut up" and frequently "inarticulate" within our society, Tillie Olsen acknowledges that for nearly *every person*, man *or* woman (save those lucky few who find themselves blessed with "enabling circumstances") there are subtle and not-so-subtle obstacles that hinder communication—obstacles that have nothing to do with one's native intelligence, one's perception of the world, one's creative nature.

Though Tillie Olsen does not identify Grammar A as one of the obstacles that keep many people silent, she does suggest such items as "The overwhelmingness of the dominant" and "The knife of the perfectionist attitude" as weapons in a society/culture that, for all sorts of reasons and motives, would like to deny the medium of the written word to many of the citizenry. And Tillie Olsen's own writing style in *Silences*—a vivid nonfiction use of Grammar B—indicates that she sees value in an alternate mode of expression to break through the silencing boundaries of a traditional style. And there is the implication, though Tillie Olsen herself does not press such a point, that Grammar A—when rigidly adhered to, when taught as the only way to write—becomes one of the "obstacles, balks, encumbrances in coming to one's own voice, vision, circumference"; that the traditional grammar of style, when it assumes total power over all "approved" writing and expression, is a "pressure toward censorship" that many teachers of English unwittingly abet: censoring out of existence all writing that does not fit into the "box" and the confines of the arbitrarily defined "well made."

Olsen's *Silences* is a liberating book in all its parts—with the following brief passage giving a good idea of what she has to say and the alternate style in which she has chosen to write it.

*   *   *

Do not forget:
      The overwhelmingness of the dominant.
      The daily saturation.
      Isolations.

The knife of the perfectionist attitude.
The insoluble.
Economic imperatives.

*How much it takes to become a writer. Bent (far more common than we
assume), circumstances, time, development of craft—but beyond that: how much
conviction as to the importance of what one has to say, one's right to say it. And the
will, the measureless store of belief in oneself to be able to come to, cleave to, find
the form for one's own life comprehensions. Difficult for any male not born into a
class that breeds such confidence. Almost impossible for a girl, a woman.*

*These pressures toward censorship, self-censorship; toward accepting, abiding by
entrenched attitudes, thus falsifying one's own reality, range, vision, truth, voice,
are extreme for women writers . . . remain a complex problem for women writing in
our time.*

To discuss and define them is, I think, of great value and importance, for
thus only can the labour be shared, the difficulties solved.

—Virginia Woolf

Fear

Fear is a powerful reason; those who are economically dependent have
strong reasons for fear. . . . But [even with economic independence]
some fear, some ancestral memory prophesying war, still remains, it
seems. . . .

What then can be the nature of the fear that still makes concealment
necessary . . . and reduces our boasted freedom to a farce? . . . Again
there are three dots; again they represent a gulf—of silence this time, of
silence inspired by fear. And since we lack both the courage to explain it
and the skill . . .

—From Woolf's great *Three Guineas*

"And here I must step warily, for already I feel the lash upon my shoul-
der."

—Virginia Woolf

Fear. How could it be otherwise, as one is also woman.

The centuries past. The other determining difference—not biology—for
woman. Constrictions, coercions, penalties for being female. Enforced. Sometimes physically enforced.

Reprisals, coercions, penalties for not remaining in what was, is, deemed
suitable in her sex.

The writer-woman is not excepted, because she writes.

Fear—the need to please, to be safe—in the literary realm too. Founded fear. Power is still in the hands of men. Power of validation, publication, approval, reputation, coercions, penalties.

"The womanhood emotion." Fear to hurt.[1]

"Liberty is the right not to lie."
"What are rights without means?"

Love

Of course it is not fear alone.

Fear—in itself—is assailable. As every revolt against oppressive power throughout the human past testifies.

There is also—love. The need to love and be loved.

It has never yet been a world right for love, for those we love, for ourselves, for flowered human life.

The oppression of women[2] is like no other form of oppression (class, color—though these have parallels). It is an oppression entangled through with human love, human need, genuine (core) human satisfactions, identifications, fulfillments.

How to separate out the chains from the bonds, the harms from the value, the truth from the lies.[3]

What compounds the personal agony for us, is that portion of the harm which comes to us from the beings we are close to, who are close to us. Their daily part in the balks, lessenings, denials. Which we must daily encounter.

And counter?

"The times are not ripe for us," the times are "not yet." Except for a privileged few who escape, who benefit from its effects, it remains a maiming sex-class-race world for ourselves, for those we love. The changes that will enable us to live together without harm ("no one's fullness of being at the cost of another's") are as yet only in the making (and we are not only beings seeking to change; changing; we are also that which our past has made us). In such circumstances, taking for one's best achievement means almost inevitably at the cost of others' needs.

(And where there are children. . . . And where there are children. . . .)

Leechings, balks, encumbrances.
Harms.

AND YET THE TREE DID—DOES—BEAR FRUIT.

---

[1]"Whenever a man [appeals to the womanhood emotion] he rouses in her, it is safe to say, a conflict of emotions of a very deep and primitive kind which it is extremely difficult for her to analyze or to reconcile."—Woolf, *Three Guineas*

[2]—which, among all else, results in our being one out of twelve in recognized achievement—

[3]Writer, as well as human, task.

PART THREE

"Graduation Brain Waves" by Laura Egbert

Written in an undergraduate composition course taught by Dr. Priscilla Tate at Texas Christian University, "Graduation Brain Waves" demonstrates the use of the alternate style to write a "theme."

--Already 8:57, and the prolific Senior class president still hasn't finished proliferating. Oh well, nothing better to do than sit in an aluminum chair for hours and hours and hours and

"now for the convocation."

There I sat, "My most memorable years; the day I'll never forget"--HIGH SCHOOL GRADUATION. Behind the artificial insincere trickles of tears, the unfamiliar formality, and the flip of a tassle, I saw the girl who entered high school in knee socks, pin curls, and baby-blue ribbons. Confronted with purple eye shadow, pink panty hose, and frosted-white hair, I realized what you had to do to grow up--Fake It:

          Wrinkle your nose
          smile
          laugh--but not too much
          drink
          smoke
          keep smiling
          keep laughing
          "What kind of sports are you interested in?"

Dates were always fun.

Especially if you did . . . date, that is. Ahhh, those proms-- invaluable experiences. Mom always said, "if you don't have a good time it doesn't really matter--it builds character you know."

          Come in . . . shake Daddy's hand and let's get out of here
          the flower doesn't match the dress
          little car grease on the dress never hurt anything
               Silence, Silence, Silence
          Get there. Dance. Sit. Doritos and Dip.
               12:01

```
What time did you say you had to be home?  I didn't.
      Silence, Silence, Silence
      fumble, fumble, fumble
            Kiss?  Forehead.
      Cry, Cry, Cry
      There, There, There
      INNOCENCE.
```

Like needles pricking my skin, I feel my foot falling asleep

again after re-crossing my legs for the fourth time.

Cute fellow--wish he didn't talk so much though/and he's said the

word "future" 27 times--I counted. It's all part of growing up I

suppose. Waiting, I mean. No more Daddy's little girl or Mama's

little helper; no more bloody knees or red-rubber-toed tennis shoes;

no more dirty finger nails or a grape juice moustashe around the

corners of your mouth.

        YOU'RE A BIG GIRL NOW!!


```
      Pooh bear and Piglet
      Nancy Drew
      Sunday school
      "Get out of my Make-Up drawer!"
      Eskimo Pies
      The Jetsons, Flintstones, and Lost in Space--WARNING WARNING!!
      "Clean up your room!"
      Piano lessons
      Ballet lessons                    UGH!
      Naps
      MATTEL
      starched crunchy petticoats
      orange fishnets with garters and Carter Starters
      pinks, blues, and Sugar & spice & everything nice.
```

Surely SOMEONE else besides me has to go to the bathroom! And

they're only on the "B's"! I'm going to trip--I just know it.

It's taking forever to get to my name. I really don't know what

I'm supposed to do. I thought I was supposed to know everything

now. I mean, after all, I'm a high school GRADUATE.

THESIS STATEMENT: Times have changed.

    --Be more specific; remember, give concrete examples--

SUCH AS: HIGH SCHOOL = UTOPIA!!

          or

WHAT HIGH SCHOOL HAS MEANT TO ME in 1000 words by Wednesday the

10th, and thank you very much.

          Dead Tunafish sandwiches
          "Stand up straight; Don't Slump!"
          Tinsel teeth
          $a^2 + b^2 = c^2$
          War is unhealthy for children and other living things.
          Jock
          Shades
          Coors
          Far-out
          Led Zepplin
          SMILE--HAVE A HAPPY DAY
          Genre
          NaCl
          George Washington, Thomas Jefferson, Honest Abe and
               all that jazz

     Yes, this _is_ a long commencement.

Yea, but it's one of those "once-in-a-lifetime-experiences."

From Daqueries to Dunkin Donuts, from Dr. Pepper to Dr. Stillman's,

from Simon to Garfunkul, I learned what it meant to be "NEETO."

But then, everyone was. (except Marsha who really didn't care one

way or the other about school much any way. Her mother thinks it's

all because she broke up with that guy with hair longer than hers,

but Tom, his best friend doesn't think so; Jodey and Beth don't

know either, but they always pretend like they do--people do a

lot of pretending, don't they?)

I'm not ready to graduate yet! I just learned how to balance

sunglasses on top of my head!

With the quick CLICK of the camera shutter, my "most memorable

years" flash before me: I can still see the white-lace hand-me-

down formal hanging dormantly in the closet, while the transparent

blue plastic hides the dull maroon, rum-scented, sparkling punch

stain; the endless memorization of Elton John's latest lyrics

"Good-Bye Yellow Brick Road" ...

      Follow the Yellow Brick Road. . .
                                    .
                               .
                           .
                       .
                     ?????

I'm next?!
You're next!
Clomp, Clomp, Clomp
Smile-Look happy; Look sad.
My cap's falling off!
swallow-breathe-sweat
stand up straight
smile
Which hand?
Diploma?
Shake hands.
Smile.

IT'S OVER.

   good.

"Ezra Pound" by Jamy Fox

Jamy Fox, a teacher of high school English in the Tulsa Public School System, wrote this Grammar B paper in a graduate seminar on Ezra Pound. Miss Fox received an "A" for her paper and was commended by the professor—a distinguished literary scholar participating in the University of Tulsa's Institute of Modern Letters—for its "great charm." It, too, demonstrates that the alternate style can be used in academe, at the highest level, to write an acceptable critical/scholarly composition. Note that the citations—referring to particular passages in Pound's various texts and to lines from Emerson and Dante—are presented not in the usual Grammar A footnote/endnote form but as quite succinct Grammar B sidenotes: PE/276, PE/251, etc. (with PE = Hugh Kenner, *The Pound Era* [Berkeley: University of California Press, 1971] and Cs = *The Cantos of Ezra Pound* [New York: New Directions, 1969]).

I

PE/276

```
        But,
            of course,
    only those who have personality and emotions
        know what it means to
            to want to escape
            from these things.
```

PE/251

```
        Concepts do not decay,
                          but    inferior minds
                          and    inferior artists
            waddle about   ----------------------.
```

Cs/570

```
    The pusillanimous wanting all men cut down to worm size.
```

PE/225

```
Metaphor, the revealer of nature. . . .
The known interprets the obscure,
the universe is alive with myth.
```

PE/239

```
        a Vortex is a circulation with a still center:
        a system of energies drawing in whatever comes
        near ("Energy creates pattern")
```

Cs/529

$$\pi\acute{\alpha}\nu\tau\alpha\ \,'\rho\epsilon\iota$$

PE/277

```
    Nothing is so unbelievable as exact truth told in
                a calm voice
```

PE/171

```
On the second of May, 1945, Ezra Pound, coming down the
salita, he thought for the last time, a pirated reprint
from Shanghai of Legge's Confucius in his coat pocket and
a dictionary of ideograms in the other . . .
```

Cs/520
521

```
    What thou lovest well remains,
                          the rest is dross
    What thou lov'st well shall not be reft from thee
    What thou lov'st well is thy true heritage . . .
```

PE/258

```
            Shape, Gaudier thought,
            manifests psychic intent
```

PE/273
```
                    the little sins
                  prepare the habit
            great sins will later gratify . . .
```

PE/460
495
```
                              T H E   C A G E
                              THE CAGE
                                thecage
```

PE/297
```
            Poor Ezra . . .
            he had a future once,      but
            he has played his cards so badly
            that I think he has barely a past now.
```

PE/173   . . . a steady preoccupation with persistently patterned energies.

Cs/623   "A man's paradise is his good nature"
```
                                  sd/ Kati.
            . . .
            having his own mind to stand by him
```

PE/185   The image . . . is a radiant node or cluster; it is what I can, and must perforce, call a VORTEX, from which, and through which, and into which, ideas are constantly rushing. . . . An <u>image</u> is real because we know it directly.

Cs/59
```
                  If a man have not order within him
            He can not spread order about him;
            . . . . .
            And he said
                  "Anyone can run to excesses,
            It is easy to shoot past the mark,
            It is hard to stand firm, in the middle."
```

PE/219 For   it must
```
        when                      composition
          the                of
            single       unit
              line   the
                is               justify
                        to           its
      contain    minute      something      separate
          some        torsion,              existence.
```

Cs/632
```
                  to enter the presence at sunrise
                  up out of hell, from the labyrinth
                        the path wide as a hair
                  &   as to mental velocities:
                        . . . . .
                        The duration
                        in re/ mental velocity
                  as to antennae
                  as to malevolence.
                        . . . . .
                        . . . Velocity.
                  Without guides, having nothing but courage
                  Shall audacity last into fortitude?
```

PE/232   Tradition is the artist's stock of capital;
it can tap impulses "older than the fish."

Cs/573   . . . In nature are signatures
                        needing no verbal tradition,

PE/157   Truth is the transference of power.

                              II

PE/239   the personal Vortex . . .
                      will draw into the artist's personal dynamism
                      his usable arraying of past Vortices.

PE/196   Composition à la mode chinoise was one of the directions
              the vers-libre movement, guided by current intuitions of
              beauty, was fated to explore . . .

PE/195   . . . he was entitled
                                    to reflect
                      that a China of the mind existed at last.

PE/273   it is always
                                               small differences
                                               that are decisive

PE/290   Metamorphosis--identity persisting through
                      change--
                                gives the rationale of "artistic unity"

PE/238   . . . Vorticism was le mot juste. It is traceable to
              Pound's figure . . . of words as electrified cones,
              charged with "the power of tradition, of centuries of
              race consciousness, of agreement, of association," an
              image . . . for all that the artist does not invent but
              must know. . . .

CW/003   of his students
                      Confucius demanded
                                    only two qualifications:

                          intelligence
                          and industry

PE/153   Luminous Details, then, are "patterned integrities" which
              transferred out of their context of origin
              retain their power to enlighten us.

PE/161   "Nature herself . . .
                          has no grammar."

PE/447   it suggested that world harmony
                      would spring from an ethic
                      a single sheet of paper could encompass. . . .

Cs/605   B u i l d e r s   h a d   k e p t   t h e   p r o p o r t i o n

PE/191   I defined the vortex
                      as "the point of maximum energy,"
                          and said that the vorticist relied on the
                                "primary pigment," and on that alone.

Cs/609   UBI AMOR IBI OCULUS EST.

Emerson   "a man cannot bury his meanings so deep in his book but
          time and like-minded men will find them."

PE/164   Nature does not use <u>pi</u>

PE/238   virtù, for the individuating energy

PE/268   . . . all the while, underneath
              ran a mystical conviction . . .
              that one might actually be
              possessed, beyond role, by
              the actual <u>virtù</u> of the great
              dead whom one has much pondered . . .

PE/215   A developed sense of probabilities,
                          often an inherited consensus of probabilities,
                      guides our understanding of all verse . . .

Cs/610   that the body of light come forth
                          from the body of fire
                  And that your eyes come to the surface
                      from the deep wherein they were sunken,

PE/241   in "doing what Nature does,"
                                  the mind generates forms . . .

PE/230   is the surest way to a fructive western idea the misunderstanding
              of an eastern one? . . .

                              III

PE/312   . . . sheer mind,
          sheer intellection of self-interfering patterns,
                  was the guarantor of all values.

CF/047   . . . the real man
                  has to look his heart in the eye
                  even when he is alone.

Cs/529   the sage
              delighteth in water
                      the humane man has amity with the hills

PE/242   Success is predictability,
          a function of the habit into which energy most often lapses.

CW/003   What tragedy that man must die
                                  feeling a failure.
                      Confucius did.

PE/267   Teaching is sharing,
                          a function of generosity. . . .

CF/051   Self-discipline is rooted in rectification of the heart

PE/200   He tried running the mood into a mask . . .

PE/445   XIII, the Canto about Kung . . . .

PE/446   Chu Hsi invented the Kung we know . . .

```
Cs/58        Kung walked

PE/230                           Is the life of the mind
                                   a history of interesting mistakes?

CF/ 33            If the root be in confusion,
                     nothing will be well governed.

Cs/575        Religion? with no dancing girls at the altar?
                     REligion?

CF/ 35   He showed his intelligence by acting straight from the heart.

Cs/521        Pull down thy vanity
                             How mean thy hates
                  Fostered in falsity
                             Pull down thy vanity,
           Rathe to destroy, niggard in charity,
           Pull down thy vanity,
                             I say pull down.

PE/241           Mind was energy, and
             "matter that has not sufficient mind to permeate it
                  grows . . . gangrenous and rotten"

Cs/118                 "Nothing we made, we set nothing in order . . ."



                                   IV

Cs/530             But in the caged panther's eyes:
                                   "Nothing.  Nothing that you can do . . ."

Cs/632                                   Velocity
                  Without guides, having nothing but courage
                  Shall audacity last into fortitude?
                       You are tender as a marshmallow, my Love,
                       I cannot use you as a fulcrum.
                          You have stirred my mind out of dust.

Cs/526                             two halves of the tally
                  but I will come out of this knowing no one
                  neither they me

PE/232   . . . A grotesque is an energy which aborts,
                                            as if to express
                  its dissatisfaction with available boundaries . . .

PE/268                       "Why try and give the impression of
                             a consistent and indivisible person-
                             ality?" . . . "I have allowed these
                             contradictory things to struggle
                             together, and the group that has
                             proved the most powerful I have fixed
                             upon as my most essential ME."

PE/273        though  he  can  only  be  what  he  is,  he  can  look  back
                  along  the  way  he  has  come  at  branching-points . . .

Cs/107             mind's attempt to invade a vacuum
```

Cs/572   . . . the squirmers plunder men's mind,
                                    want all men cut down to worm-size.

Cs/530   Nor can who has passed a month in the death cells
                                believe in capital punishment
                            No man who has passed a month in the death cells
                                believes in cages for beasts

PE/288   . . . appalling energies expended against appalling obtuseness . . .

PE/222   Emotion is born out of habit.

Cs/576   Old crocks to die in a bug-house:

Cs/521   "Pull down thy vanity, I say pull down . . . . "

PE/216   Time and again the only meaning of "correct" is "traditional. . . ."

PE/251   Concepts do not decay . . .

PE/228   Ingenuity can go a long way toward sustaining such a case,
            so adept is a mind seeking relevance. . . .

Cs/521   But to have done instead of not doing
                                    this is not vanity
                            To have, with decency, knocked

PE/226   Give it time, and Pound's flywheel always restored a balance. . . .

CF/051   . . . you enrich and irrigate the character
                            by the process of looking straight into
                            the heart and then acting on the results.
                            Thus the mind becomes your palace and the
                            body can be at ease . . .

PE/276   Poetry is not a turning loose of emotion,
                            but an escape from emotion;
                                    it is not the expression of personality,
                                            but an escape from personality.

PE/218   Where there is no tradition at all, we may learn
                            humility from the luckless scholar who saw reason
                            to approach the Linear B script by way of Basque,
                            and eventually derived elegiac poems from what
                            are now taken to be storehouse inventories. . . .

Dante   That day we went no further

PART FOUR

"Rhetorical Malnutrition in Prelim Questions and Literary Criticism" by Donald C. Stewart

Donald C. Stewart, a professor of English at Kansas State University, has long been concerned with teaching English composition in the classroom. His publications include *The Authentic Voice: A Pre-Writing Approach to Student Writing* and a variety of articles and stories. He has served on the editorial board of the National Council of Teachers of English.

In the following article, "Rhetorical Malnutrition in Prelim Questions and Literary Criticism," originally published in *College English* (October, 1977), Professor Stewart speaks from the perspective of the professional writer/educator about the need in contemporary English teaching and academic writing for a greater understanding of style—in all its "grammars" and variations. Professor Stewart's article helps place our discussion of an alternate style in a meaningful and rewarding context.

*   *   *

Before embarking on a topic as presumptuous as my title suggests, I offer these disclaimers. To generalize definitely on prelim questions and scholarly articles, I would have had to read all that have been written for at least the last ten years. How would I ever collect that material, much less read it? Surely, even the most determined pedant would hesitate before undertaking an enterprise of that scope. Since I have no pedant credentials, and seek none, I reduced the project to manageable size by collecting random samples of prelim questions and scholarly articles. At the appropriate times I will indicate the size and nature of each sample. For the sake of my generalizations, I hope, of course, that the samples are representative of the larger mass of data from which they were extracted.

The sample of prelim questions is not as uniform as I would have liked. Because of the depressed job market for Ph.D.'s in English, many departments have cut back and considerably altered their doctoral programs in the last three or four years. Some of them sent questions from the era ending about 1972 or 1973. Others which have developed programs tailored to the needs and interests of specific students sent questions used in examinations since 1974. What I have to say about the rhetoric of these questions will not, however, be significantly altered by these differences in the context in which the questions were given.

Readers who anticipate a detailed Aristotelian or Ciceronian analysis of the rhetoric of particular questions will be disappointed. Prelims, as we all recognize, are an early albeit traumatic rite of passage for the potential scholar. Their significance diminishes rapidly once one has passed them. I was interested, therefore, only in the organizational paradigms generated by

121

the majority of the questions, paradigms which might anticipate those in the writing of mature scholars. At this point, I discovered a gap in my data which I could not repair. I needed the answers to the questions to see whether or not my expectations about them were accurate. Clearly, I could never get those answers. However, I have taught enough literature and composition courses over the last twenty-five years to develop a good sense of the response a question will generate from a student.

Now to the prelim questions. I asked the directors of graduate studies in English at twenty-eight public and private universities in all sections of the country to send me representative questions. Despite the fact that only eighteen of the twenty-eight responded to my request, and of these only thirteen supplied questions, I received 599 questions. If I have overlooked some particularly brilliant rhetorical sequences or felicitous single questions, I attribute this failure of insight on my part to the numbing effect of reading these almost 600 questions.

My primary interest, again, was in predicting the kind of paradigm these questions would generate. It did not take me very long to find a clear pattern. Sometimes with limited amounts of material, sometimes with masses of material complexly presented, students were asked to define, compare and contrast, generalize and support, argue, examine, explicate, discriminate, evaluate, and inevitably, at several points in their exams, to "discuss" specific works or groups of works, authors, singly or in groups, and passages from major critical works. These variations were superficial, however. Most of these questions forced the student into a single paradigm: thesis statement, supporting generalizations and examples, conclusion. I would be willing to bet that Ph.D. candidates retreat into this paradigm as hastily and as predictably as freshmen retreat into the five paragraph essay, the one safe form which will get them a passing grade in composition courses.

Only the "discuss" questions offered the candidates a reasonable chance of an alternative, but it must have been a brave one who ventured outside the traditional route in answering his/her questions. So predominant was the demand for the single paradigm I have mentioned that I began searching diligently for any question which elicited some paradigm other than the thesis statement, supporting generalizations, and conclusion. All I found were two impossible questions (the "discuss all human knowledge" kind), and a few open-ended questions which either did not implicitly elicit answers already known by the examiner, or which offered the candidate opportunities to employ alternative paradigms in answering them. For example: "You have just been assigned the task of ordering books for Eliot studies at a brand new library which has no Eliot section at all. What primary and secondary works would you order? Defend your selections." This kind of question, I believe, permits the candidate freedom to select his/her material and put a shape on it that he/she desires, for the evaluation of examiners who are looking, hopefully, for possibilities they might not have considered. Another technique for generating innovative rhetorical paradigms might be to present the candidate with a research problem which the examiner is working on and has not solved. (Richard Altick's *The Scholar Adventurers* [New York: The Free Press, 1950] is a gold mine of suggestions of the kinds of problems which troubled literary scholars for decades.) While it is doubtful that any candidate could solve a particular problem because the student would lack the examiner's total familiarity with it, he/she might suggest methods of attack which the examiner, despite vigorous attempts to review all possibilities, had over-looked. More to my point, such a question might elicit a dynamic paradigm, one revealing the mind thinking, not having arrived at its conclusions and delivering them cold.

Two issues of importance, rhetorical alternatives to the standard paradigm and the connection between a student's answers to prelim questions and the paradigms she/he adopts as a writer of scholarly articles, I recognize here, but I wish to postpone discussion of them until after my review of scholarly articles, to which I now turn. How serious is the problem of rhetorical malnutrition in their organizational paradigms? To get my answers, and again I remind readers that they are extremely tentative because they develop from limited data, I examined the general rhetorical structure of 109 articles in 19 scholarly magazines. Most of these were Spring or Summer, 1975, issues, the oldest being one publication dated April, 1974. The magazines were ones which are well known: *PMLA*, *American Literature*, *Philological Quarterly*, *Nineteenth Century Fiction*, *Studies in English Literature*, *Modern Philology*, etc. Some are more prestigious than others, but all are among the most widely read journals by specialists in the fields they represent.

I offer no criticisms of the scholarship supporting these papers. It seemed to me consistently thorough and intelligent. And I have tried to avoid duplicating observations already made in past decades by others whose interest in the content and style of scholarly articles in English is different from mine.[1] However, I did notice a few relatively superficial matters which deserve passing comment. For example, we have an occasional writer who cannot resist the impulse to descend into sociologese: "The significance of Poe's ratiocinative phase can perhaps be best understood in the context of his broader thematic concerns." Others, not necessarily sixteenth century specialists, have yet to escape the influence of John Lyly: "Samson is not primarily the hero who suffers or the hero who resists temptation but the hero

---

[1]See Richard Altick, *The Art of Literary Research* (New York, 1963: W. W. Norton & Co.), pp. 181–202; R. B. McKerrow, "Form and Matter in the Publication of Research," *RES*, 16 (1940), 116–21, reprinted in *PMLA*, 65 (1950), 3–8; Samuel Eliot Morison, "History as a Literary Art" in *By Land and By Sea* (New York, 1953; Knopf), pp. 289–98; Jacques Barzun & Henry F. Graff, *The Modern Researcher* (New York, 1957: Harcourt, Brace & World), pp. 229–287; Wallace W. Douglas, "Souls Among Masterpieces: The Solemn Style of Modern Critics," *American Scholar*, 23 (Winter, 1953/54), 43–55. I am indebted to Altick for directing me to these publications.

who etc. etc." And from this same writer we get "Samson understands that his duty and his fulfillment is to act in accordance with the will of God; his problem, at once spiritual, moral, intellectual, and practical is etc. etc." Some writers, like the inveterate "whicher" whom Thurber castigates in his "Ladies and Gentleman's Guide to Good English," keep tweeting these "at once's" at one all the way through their papers. Other stylistic affectations which occur persistently are the "in a sense, then," "in short" (but never "in long"), "the significance of X's Y can be best be understood in the context of," "let it be noted that," "at any rate," etc. But this digression is but to whet my already blunted purpose.

I was interested primarily to discover whether or not writers, once free from the pressures of time and anxiety of preliminary examinations, experimented freely with expository forms. For the most part, they did not. The articles I read repeated, with mind numbing consistency, a pattern of organization which varies only when some of these components are omitted or slightly rearranged: (1) statement of the problem; (2) review of the relevant scholarship; (3) statement of method in discussing the problem; (4) analysis of evidence to support generalizations; (5) conclusion. Sometimes the first three items are collapsed into a single paragraph (particularly by Canadian and English writers); sometimes they are extended over two to five paragraphs, sometimes several pages, as part of a first section in the article. But most of the time they are there.

Surely there is a paradox in the fact that those who write—about the novel, which continually defies the efforts of our best critical minds to generalize successfully about its form; the play; and the sonnet, the lyric, the epic, the epistle, the haiku, the ode—restrict themselves most of the time to one expository form.

Why do writers of scholarly articles retreat into a sterile and unimaginative paradigm again and again and again? (Incidentally, as will become increasingly apparent, I do not accept the notion that the standard paradigm is always the best and most efficient way for us to deliver to readers the fruits of our literary scholarship.) I would suggest two reasons. The first, admittedly a conjecture, has to do with a question posed earlier: the connection between the answers students write for prelim questions and the kinds of scholarly articles they write after they enter the profession. Typical graduate students in English have been drilled, either in high school or in freshman college courses to produce some form of the five paragraph essay (our modern streamlining of the classical five part discourse, developed by the ancient rhetoricians and disseminated widely in the nineteenth century by the popularity of Hugh Blair's *Lectures on Rhetoric and Belle Lettres*). If they become graduate teaching assistants, as most do, they get further reinforcement in this pattern, or one like it, because they teach it. Because most are candidates for degrees in literature, their knowledge of composition history and current theory is virtually nonexistent. Therefore, when writing, they produce what they have always produced without any awareness of alternative paradigms. Second, editors of scholarly magazines in English apparently favor that kind of work. Perhaps scholars become so accustomed to writing that way that they do it reflexively. But I think the real reasons are much deeper than that and infinitely more profound. Those of us who attempt to keep up with the leading edge of composition research and theory are now aware that we are posed on the edge of a frontier which opens out into a compositional territory that is vast and unexplored. A few hardy souls have preceded us into this wilderness, but more now are taking courage to venture forth.

In the space provided here I have time only to suggest briefly the reasons why we have come to this particular frontier and to adumbrate the nature of the terrain ahead. One finds in the early 1960s some significant challenges to our whole conception of the nature of good writing. Francis Christensen's cumulative sentence was an attempt to free us from the tyranny of the periodic sentence. The latter, readers will remember, he characterizes as best suitable for delivering knowledge cold. But the cumulative sentence, he tells us, "does not represent the idea as conceived, pondered over, reshaped, packaged, and delivered cold. It is *dynamic* [italics mine] rather than static, representing the mind thinking. . . . Thus, the mere form of the sentence generates ideas. It serves the needs of both the writer and the reader, the writer by compelling him to examine his thought, the reader by letting him into the writer's thought."[2] In 1964 Gordon Rohman and Albert Wlecke published their work on pre-writing, the principal thrust of which was to direct attention away from the finished product of writing and toward the process which produced it. Drawing on the work of Jerome Bruner, they had directed their attention to the ways the mind collects data and forms concepts prior to manipulating them in discourse. In some ways their work echoes the thought of Vassar's Gertrude Buck who, at the turn of the century, was trying to enrich rhetorical theory with insights from psychology and biology. For example, in her discussions of sentence grammar, she articulates again and again the point that thought, and then spoken or written discourse, begins as an inchoate mass which, upon certain stimuli, is differentiated into discrete parts. Thus, a moment of surprise begins with the interjection "Oh!" quickly followed by an "How you scared me!", the sentence unit containing subject and agent, both of which are capable of further differentiation. The point is that both Buck in 1898 and Rohman and Wlecke in 1964 were developing an organic and dynamic concept of composing.[3]

---

[2]Francis Christensen, *Notes Toward a New Rhetoric* (New York: Norton, 1967), pp. 5, 6.
[3]See Gertrude Buck, "The Psychological Significance of the Parts of Speech," *Education*, 18 (January, 1898), 269–277; D. Gordon Rohman & Albert Wlecke, "Pre-Writing: The Construction and Application of Models for Concept Formation in Writing," Cooperative Research Project No. 2174, Michigan State, 1964.

Developments in the last ten years have been even more revolutionary. Scarcely anyone interested in composition theory has not read Robert Zoellner's controversial behavioral monograph in the January, 1969, issue of *College English.* Zoellner was also concerned with process, and he added a new dimension: physical behavior and the ways it informs the entire composing process. I have read only two accounts which adequately explain the intensity of the hostility to Zoellner's work: "Mentalizing S. R. Rodent," *College English,* Nov. 1969, 215–230, by Zoellner himself, and "Paradigms and Problems: Needed Research in Rhetorical Invention," a paper delivered by Richard Young of Michigan at the 1975 Buffalo Conference on Composing. Significantly both look back to Thomas Kuhn's *The Structure of Scientific Revolutions (International Encyclopedia of Unified Science,* vols. 1 & 2, Chicago: University of Chicago Press, 1962). The key insights here, for our purposes, are Kuhn's discussions of the way paradigms shape and direct research in a number of scientific fields, and the fact that genuine revolutions occur when someone challenges the basic paradigm in which those in a particular discipline think. The process is never instantaneous. It is more a cumulation of events and frustrations among experimenters who find that the paradigm in which they are working simply is not adequate to account for recurring anomalies. An obvious historical example, one on which Kuhn himself has written, is the Copernican revolution which occurred at a time, according to Kuhn, when Ptolemaic astronomy had become a scandal.

What has all of this to do with literary criticism and composition theory? Simply this. The form in which most literary criticism is written is a fixed part of a deeply rooted paradigm which those who write are reluctant to modify or experiment with. It may be a suitable paradigm for a scientist reporting conclusions derived from empirical studies, but it is not always suitable for a humanistic discipline. Missing is the act of discovery, shared by both writer and reader, in interpretation. This paradigm has the effect of reducing the living work of great writers to museum specimens either stuffed and mounted or preserved in formaldehyde. It may even shield us from insights which another, less rigid paradigm, might generate.

One might ask the question, does the form accurately represent the way discoveries about literature occur? Often, good scholarship results from reading and re-reading which yields accumulations of insights—in no systematic way. A felt need, to recover both the experience of these discoveries and the intensity of imaginative creation, may be motivating the recent interest in performance criticism.

But lest we be carried away by the poignancy of all this, let me insist that James, like Frost, probably had, at the terrible depths of creative power, "a *hell* of a good time doing it"—there at his desk, there at the cemetery arranging the scene for the desk, there even in his room dying when he dictated his last ruminations. What is literary criticism to do with something so wonderful, with writing as an act of keeping alive rather than an image of life or of living? Or let's forget literary criticism and ask what in the teaching of literature one can do with the phenomenon of performance. It seems to me that one way literature can and should be taught is in conjunction with other kinds of performance—with dance, music, film, sports—and that a comparative analysis of modes of performance may indeed keep literary study alive in the face of the competition now before it. We must begin to begin again with the most elementary and therefore toughest questions: what it must have felt like to do this—not to mean anything, but to do it. I think anyway that that's where the glory lies: not in the tragedy but in the gayety of Hamlet and Lear and of dry-eyed Shakespeare. Indeed who knows if for Shakespeare there was even any dread to be transfigured. Maybe he took a beginning and it took him, as "germs" will do, and off they went.[4]

Poirier's emphasis here, away from analysis and toward synthesis, a recapturing of the creative act, had been prepared for by Walter Slatoff's *With Respect to Readers* (Ithaca: Cornell University Press, 1970), a book, as far as I can judge, as important as it is little read. His opening chapter makes the obvious point that works of literature exist to be read, but continues with the provocative observation that much of our teaching of literature conducts itself as if this were not so. He is particularly concerned with formalist criticism which insists on study of the work of art as a separate self-defining object. Such criticism, he asserts, can provide us with a large vocabulary for discussing a work of art and a variety of techniques for assembling an almost unlimited amount of information about it, but unfortunately, it treats the interaction of reader and work, the most significant part of any literary–aesthetic experience as if it were peripheral. "We must try," he says.

> . . . to escape from a set of related polarities and dichotomies which have seriously limited our thinking and observation: objective–subjective, clear thinking–emotional involvement, judgment–sympathy, impersonal–personal, accurate–impressionistic, knowledge–appreciation. In each of these polarities and others like them an activity associated with emotion, feeling, or involvement is seen as some kind of distortion or enemy of proper understanding. (p. 36)

It is not surprising, therefore, that Slatoff concludes by observing that

---

[4]Richard Poirier, *The Performing Self* (New York: Oxford University Press, 1971), p. 51.

. . . insofar as we divorce the study of literature from the experience of
reading and view literary works as objects to be analyzed rather than
human expressions to be reacted to; insofar as we view them as providing
order, pattern, and beauty, as opposed to challenge and disturbance;
insofar as we favor form over content, objectivity over subjectivity, de-
tachment over involvement, theoretical over real readers; insofar as we
worry more about incorrect responses than insufficient ones; insofar as we
emphasize the distinctions between literature and life rather than their
interpenetrations, we reduce the power of literature and protect ourselves
from it. (pp. 167, 168)

The point toward which I am obviously working is simply this: the
standard paradigm in literary criticism reinforces the polarities and patterns of
inadequate response which Slatoff discusses. What is needed is some alternative so that we are not bound always by this paradigm but may range freely
from it, even in literary criticism, when the subject, audience, situation, or
any combination of these factors demands it.

At the time I wrote the first draft of this essay, in the fall of 1975, I had
reached a brick wall, a situation in which I felt a need I could not satisfy, the
recognition that such a paradigm probably existed and would be useful but
that I did not know it. In January, 1976, in *Freshman English News*, Winston
Weathers' "Grammars of Style: New Options in Composition" appeared. I
feel perfectly safe in saying that this essay is one of the half dozen or so articles
on composition theory and methodology published in the last thirty years
which are landmarks. The irony of it is that those who most need to read it
would not understand it if they did. As part of my conclusion, however, I am
going to suggest the main features of this article because they speak directly to
the subject of my paper.

Two quotations from the first section of Weathers' essay will establish the
background against which he develops his new options.

What I've been taught to construct is: the well-made box. I have been
taught to put "what I have to say" into a container that is always remarkably the same, that—in spite of varying decorations—keeps to a
basically conventional form: a solid bottom, four upright sides, a fine-
fitting lid. Indeed, I may be free to put "what I have to say" in the plain
box or in the ornate box, in the large box or the small box, in the fragile
box or in the sturdy box. But always *the box*—squarish or rectangular.
And I begin to wonder if there isn't somewhere a round box or oval box
or tubular box, if somewhere there isn't some sort of container (1) that
will allow me to package "what I have to say" without trimming my
"content" to fit into a particular compositional mode, (2) that will
actually encourage me to discover new "things to say" because of the very
opportunity a newly-shaped container gives me, (3) that will be more

suitable perhaps to my own mental processes, and (4) that will provide me with a greater rhetorical flexibility, allowing me to package what I have to say in more ways than one and thus reach more audiences than one. (p. 1)

But composition teachers have not offered a number of different "boxes."

Our assumption—regardless of liberality so far as diversity of styles is concerned—is that every composition must be well-organized and unified, must demonstrate logic, must contain well-developed paragraphs; that its structure will manifest a beginning, middle, and end [Sheridan Baker has sold 1,000,000 copies of his book pushing that point of view]; that the composition will reveal identifiable types of order; that so far as the composition deals with time it will reveal a general diachronicity; etc. Our teaching and texts will be concerned, almost without exception, with "subject and thesis," "classification and order," "beginning and ending," "expansion," "continuity," "emphasis," and the like. All remains, in other words, within a particular grammar of style that leads to compositions that "make sense." (p. 2)

In contrast to this Weathers offers an alternate grammar of style which he argues has been present in Anglo-American writing for some time, in the works of Laurence Sterne, William Blake, D. H. Lawrence, James Joyce, Virginia Woolf, John Barth, Donald Barthelme, Tom Wolfe, and others. It is not primarily rational, logical, or ordered. Instead, it is often the very opposite. Its principal features are the crot, "an autonomous unit, characterized by the absence of any transitional devices that might relate it to preceding or subsequent crots," labyrinthine sentences and sentence fragments, lists, double-voices, repetitions/repetends/refrains, synchronicity (particularly noticeable in Joyce's or Woolf's work where linear prose is shaped to produce an effect of vertical time), and collage/montage.

Weathers does not argue that his new grammar should replace the old one; he sees it as a means of enriching our rhetorical options in discourse.

If we'd spend less time trying to "protect" the language from "misuse," and spend more time opening our own minds to all the things language can do and is doing, we'd be better off. . . . The art of composition finally does have something to do with the art of life. Our verbal compositions become emblematic of and analogous to our social and political "compositions." If we come to composition with options, openmindedness, adaptability, we not only fulfill ourselves the more but we obviously are capable of giving more to others. (p. 18)

Whatever direction we take, this much is clear. If the articles I have read recently are typical of scholarship in English, then we as a profession are guilty of imaginative sterility. I am not persuaded that general literary magazines, which favor somewhat informal essays not appropriate for scholarly magazines, serve as an outlet for the kind of writing I would like to see tried. And, while it is possible for some writers like Altick to enliven the traditional paradigm with a style that is fresh and vigorous, they are exceptions. In the hands of most writers the traditional paradigm generates the stylistic affectations which make much scholarly writing sleep-inducing. Is it possible that we really can do no creative thinking about the forms of expository prose? In the light of Weathers' essay, that is a rhetorical question. But inattention to these forms suggests that many writers of the scholarly articles I examined either do not know of or refuse to recognize the existence or importance of scholarship in composition and rhetoric which would have a direct influence on the work they are producing.

I conclude on an anticlimactic note. Having discovered this impoverishment in our scholarly writing and experiencing a compulsion to attack it, I decided to check my own work. I have written very little literary criticism, perhaps because instinctively I have been resisting a kind of prose which puts me in jail. But the rebel stands accused. Among the papers I have written I found the very paradigm which I have been discrediting. Surely, this is a case of the leper discovering the disease in everyone but himself until the last moment. But, at least I know now that I have it. I wonder how many others are so enlightened?

Suggested Readings: Toward Grammar B

BLAKE, WILLIAM. "The Marriage of Heaven and Hell," *The Collected Poetry and Prose of William Blake,* ed. David B. Eerdman. Garden City: Doubleday, 1965.

CAGE, JOHN. *Silence.* Middletown, Conn.: The Wesleyan University Press, 1961.

CUMMINGS, E. E. *I: Six Nonlectures.* Cambridge, Mass.: Harvard University Press, 1962.

———. *Selected Letters,* ed. F. W. Dupee and George Stade. New York: Harcourt, Brace & World, Inc., 1969.

DONAGHUE, DENIS. "For Brevity's Sake," *Saturday Review,* March 3, 1979.

DORR, PRISCILLA DIAZ. "The Ballet: Some Reflections," *Clique,* Vol. I, No. 2 (March, 1980).

GASS, WILLIAM. *On Being Blue.* Boston: Godine, 1976.

GILLIATT, PENELOPE. "About Rebellion: Two Fine Documentaries," *The New Yorker,* May 16, 1977.

HAMMARSKJÖLD, DAG. *Markings.* New York: Alfred A. Knopf, 1965.

LAWRENCE, D. H. *Sea and Sardinia.* New York: The Viking Press, 1963.

———. *Studies in Classic American Literature.* London: Heinemann, 1924.

OATES, JOYCE CAROL. "How I Contemplated the World from the Detroit House of Correction and Began My Life Over Again," *TriQuarterly,* Spring, 1969.

OLSEN, TILLIE. *Silences.* New York: Delacorte, 1978.

SARGEANT, WINTHROP. "A Head for an Eye; or, Fashion Finals in 'The Other Side of Midnight,' " *The New Yorker,* July 11, 1977.

STEIN, GERTRUDE. *How Writing Is Written,* ed. Robert B. Haas. Los Angeles: Black Sparrow Press, 1974.

TROW, GEORGE W. S. "I Cover Carter," *The New Yorker,* July 25, 1977.

UPDIKE, JOHN. *Assorted Prose.* New York: Knopf, 1965.

VONNEGUT, JR., KURT. *Welcome to the Monkey House.* New York: Delacorte, 1968.

WILLIAMS, WILLIAM CARLOS. *The Embodiment of Knowledge.* New York: New Directions, 1974.

———. *In the American Grain.* New York: New Directions, 1956.

WOLFE, TOM. *The Kandy Kolored Tangerine Flake Streamline Baby.* New York: Farrar, Straus & Giroux, 1965.